Piano•Vocal•Guitar

2nd Edition

Acoustic Classics

ISBN 978-1-4950-9817-8

HAL•LEONARD®

7777 W. BLUEMOUND RD. P.O. BOX 13819 MILWAUKEE, WI 53213

Visit Hal Leonard Online at
www.halleonard.com

CONTENTS

AMERICAN PIE

Words and Music by
DON McLEAN

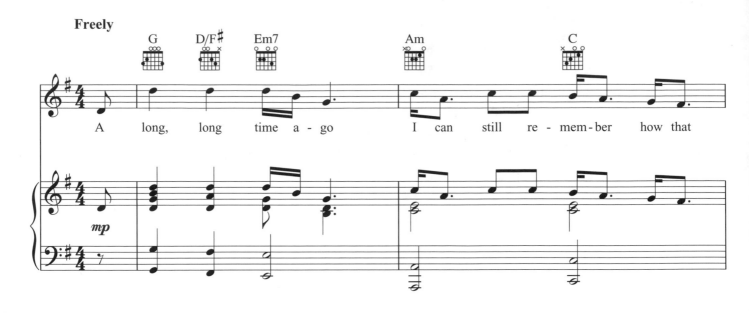

A long, long time a-go I can still re-mem-ber how that

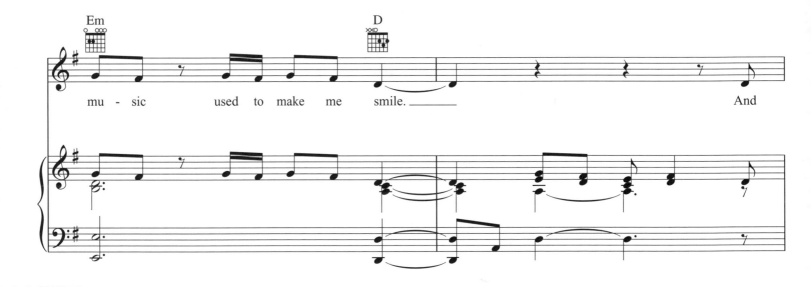

mu - sic used to make me smile. _____ And

I knew if I had my chance that I could make those peo - ple dance and

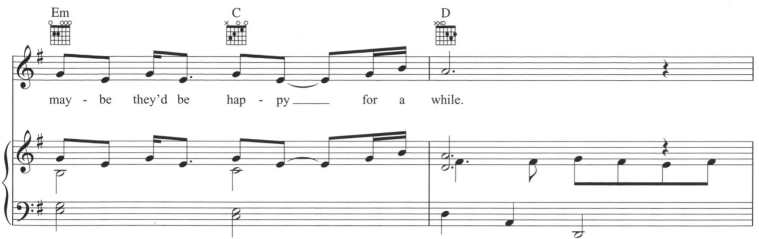

may - be they'd be hap - py ____ for a while.

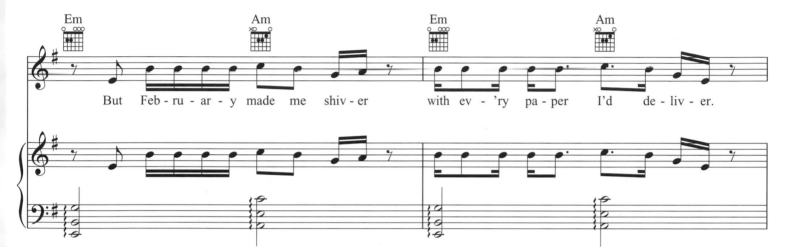

But Feb - ru - ar - y made me shiv - er with ev - 'ry pa - per I'd de - liv - er.

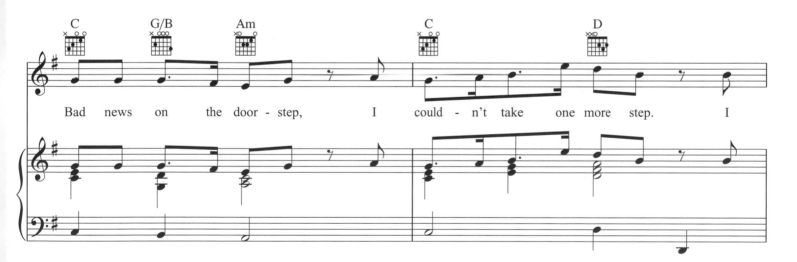

Bad news on the door - step, I could - n't take one more step. I

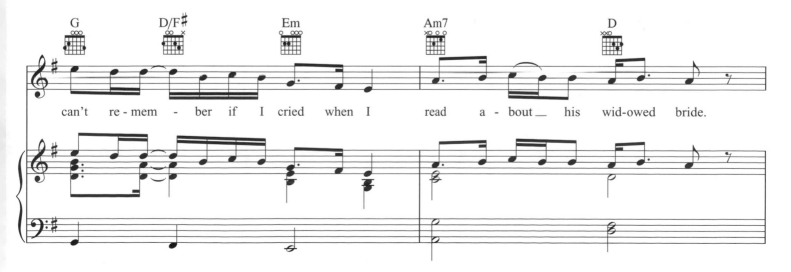

can't re - mem - ber if I cried when I read a - bout ____ his wid - owed bride.

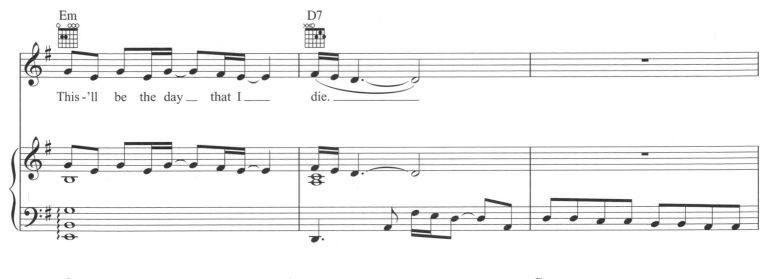

This-'ll be the day __ that I __ die. __

1. Did you __ write the book of love __ and do you __ have faith in
2.–4. *(See additional lyrics)*

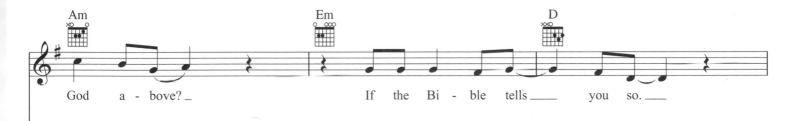

God a - bove? __ If the Bi - ble tells __ you so. __

Now do you __ be - lieve __ in rock and roll? __ Can

mu - sic   save   your   mor - tal   soul ___   and   can   you   teach   me

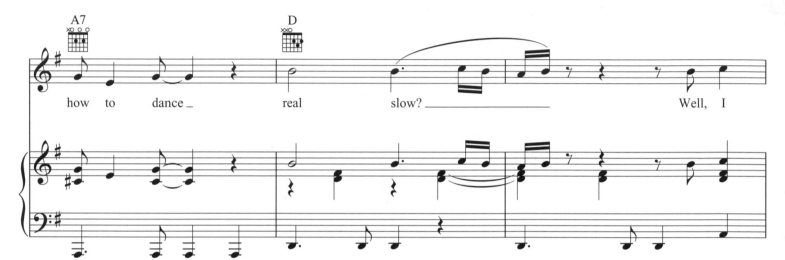

how   to   dance _   real   slow? _____   Well,   I

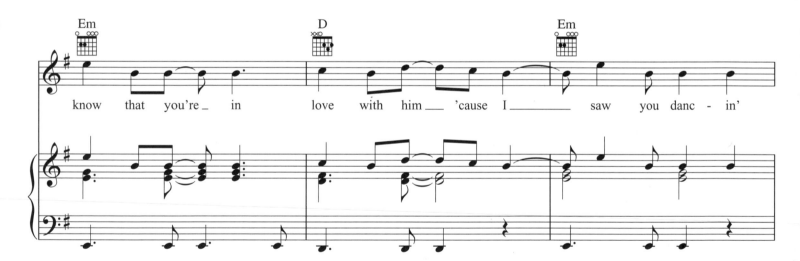

know   that   you're _   in   love   with   him ___   'cause   I _____   saw   you   danc - in'

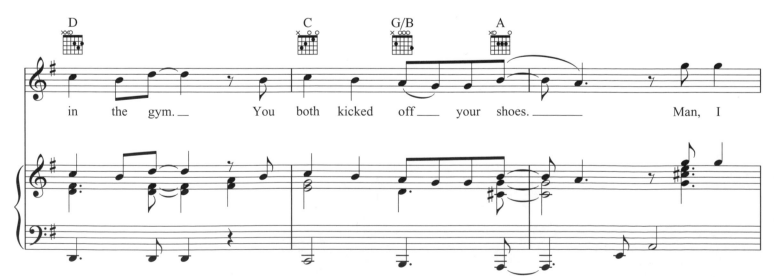

in   the   gym. __   You   both   kicked   off ___   your   shoes. _____   Man,   I

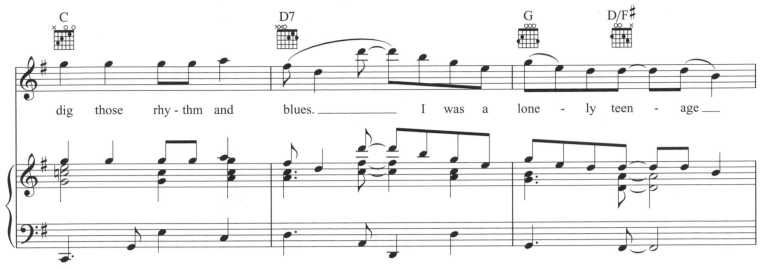

dig those rhy-thm and blues._____ I was a lone-ly teen-age___

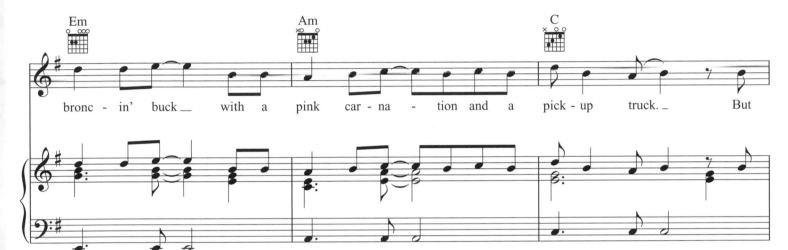

bronc-in' buck___ with a pink car-na-tion and a pick-up truck.___ But

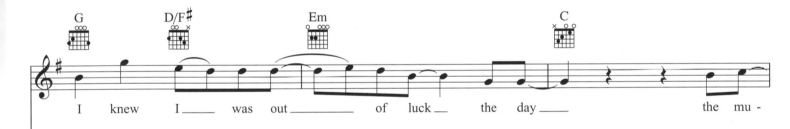

I knew I___ was out_____ of luck___ the day___ the mu-

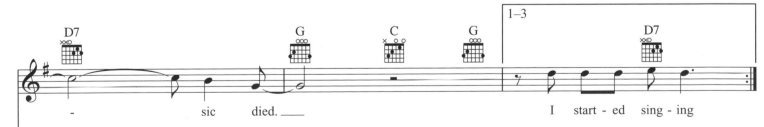

-sic died.___ I start-ed sing-ing

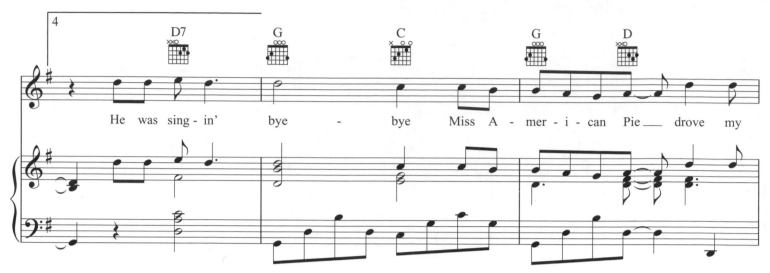

He was sing-in' bye - bye Miss A - mer - i - can Pie___ drove my

Chev-y to the lev-ee but the lev-ee was dry.___ Them

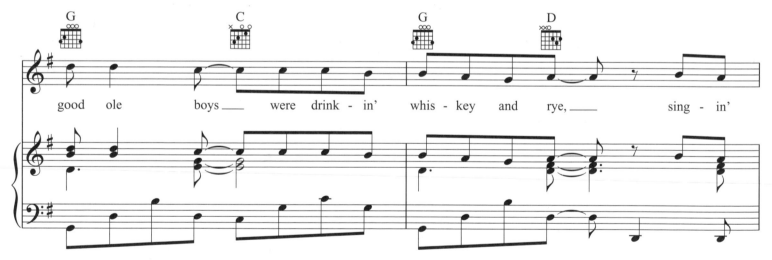

good ole boys___ were drink-in' whis-key and rye,___ sing-in'

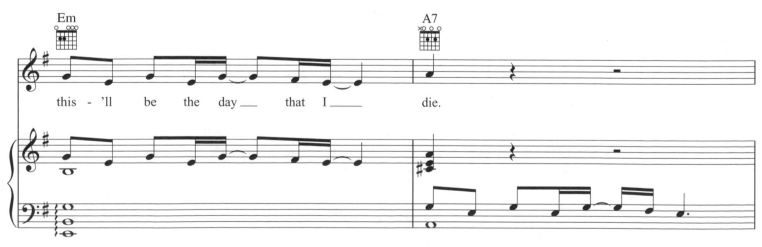

this -'ll be the day___ that I___ die.

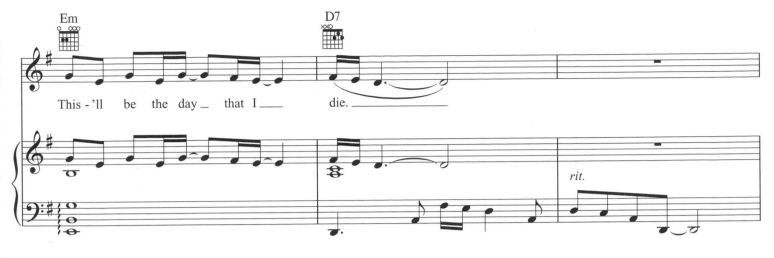

This-'ll be the day ___ that I ___ die. ___

Freely

I met a girl who sang ___ the blues ___ and I asked her for some hap-py news, ___ but

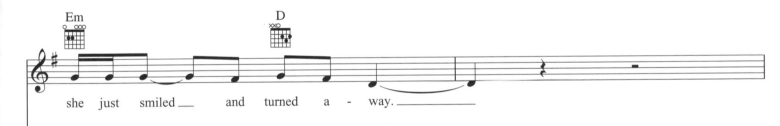

she just smiled ___ and turned a - way. ___

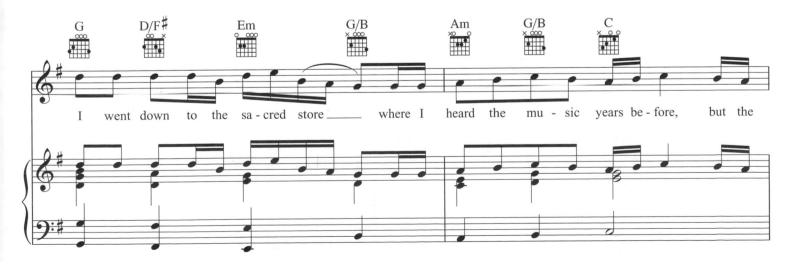

I went down to the sa-cred store ___ where I heard the mu - sic years be - fore, but the

man there said the mu-sic would-n't play. _____ And

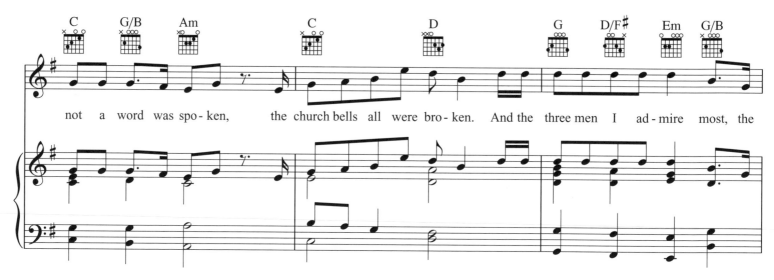

in the streets the chil-dren screamed, _ the lov-ers cried _ and the po-ets dreamed. _ But

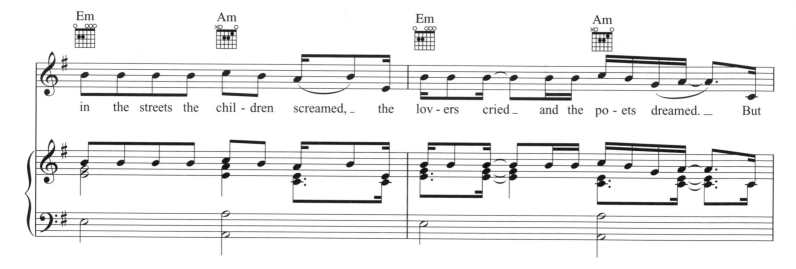

not a word was spo-ken, the church bells all were bro-ken. And the three men I ad-mire most, the

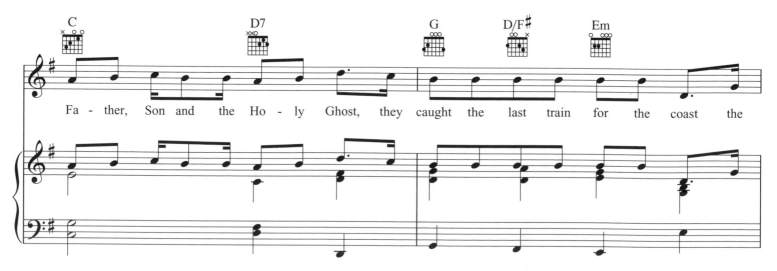

Fa - ther, Son and the Ho - ly Ghost, they caught the last train for the coast the

day the mu - sic died. And they were sing - in'

CODA this - 'll be the day __ that I ___ die. ___

Additional Lyrics

2. Now for ten years we've been on our own,
And moss grows fat on a rollin' stone
But that's not how it used to be
When the jester sang for the king and queen
In a coat he borrowed from James Dean
And a voice that came from you and me
Oh and while the king was looking down,
The jester stole his thorny crown
The courtroom was adjourned,
No verdict was returned
And while Lenin read a book on Marx
The quartet practiced in the park
And we sang dirges in the dark
The day the music died
We were singin'...bye-bye...etc.

3. Helter-skelter in the summer swelter
The birds flew off with a fallout shelter
Eight miles high and fallin' fast,
It landed foul on the grass
The players tried for a forward pass,
With the jester on the sidelines in a cast
Now the half-time air was sweet perfume
While the sergeants played a marching tune
We all got up to dance
But we never got the chance
'Cause the players tried to take the field,
The marching band refused to yield
Do you recall what was revealed
The day the music died
We started singin'... bye-bye...etc.

4. And there we were all in one place,
A generation lost in space
With no time left to start again
So come on, Jack be nimble, Jack be quick,
Jack Flash sat on a candlestick
'Cause fire is the devil's only friend
And as I watched him on the stage
My hands were clenched in fits of rage
No angel born in hell
Could break that Satan's spell
And as the flames climbed high into the night
To light the sacrificial rite
I saw Satan laughing with delight
The day the music died
He was singin'...bye-bye...etc.

ANGIE

Words and Music by MICK JAGGER
and KEITH RICHARDS

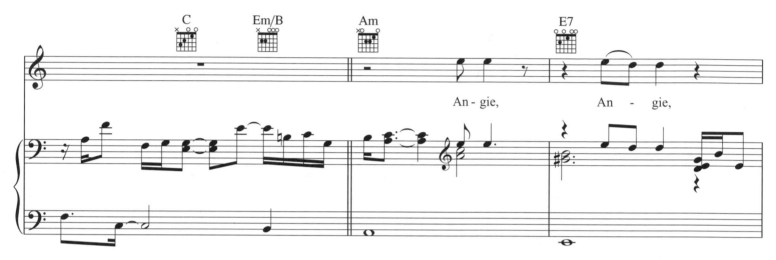

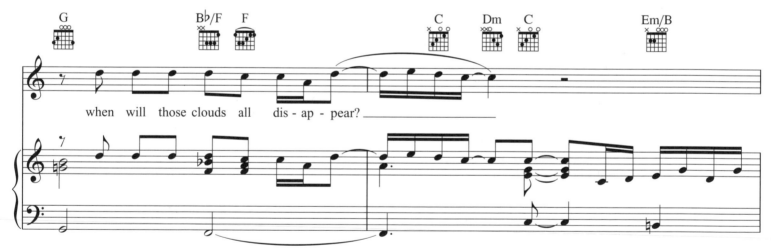

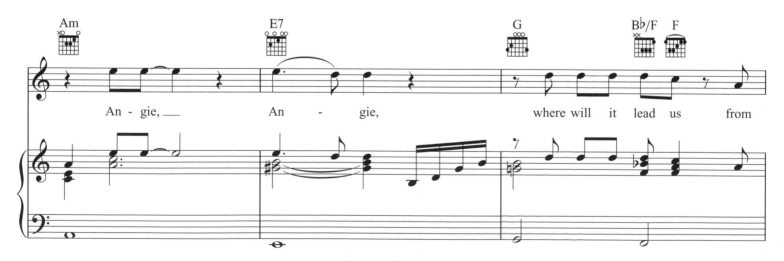

here? _____ With no lov-ing in our souls _ and no

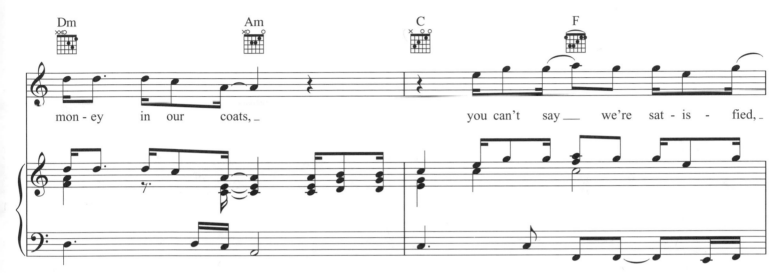

mon-ey in our coats, _ you can't say _ we're sat-is-fied, _

but, An-gie,

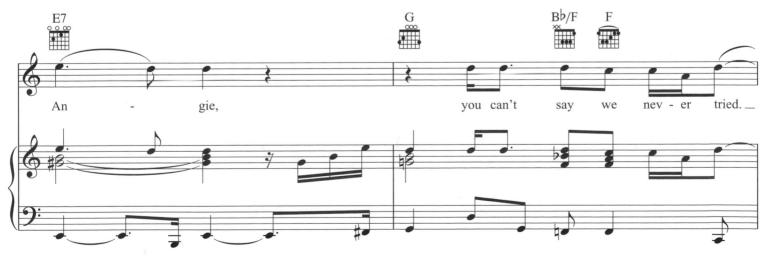

An - gie, you can't say we nev-er tried. _

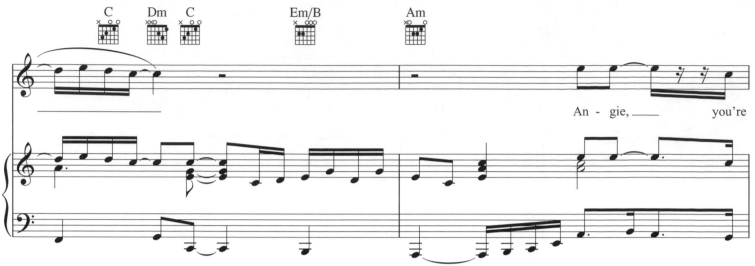

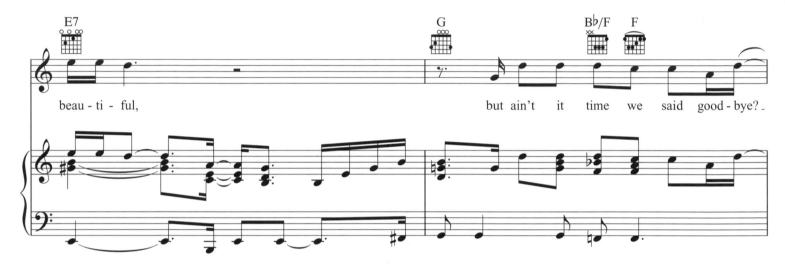

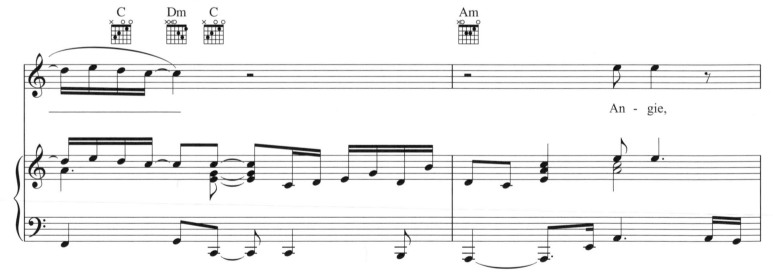

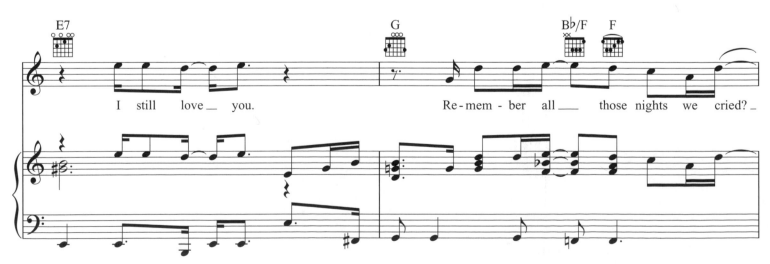

All the dreams we held_ so close_ seemed to all_

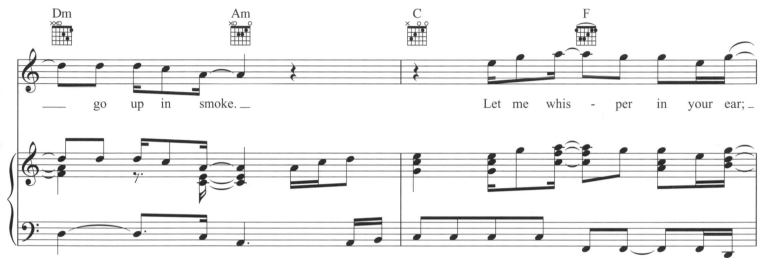

_ go up in smoke. _ Let me whis - per in your ear; _

"An - gie,

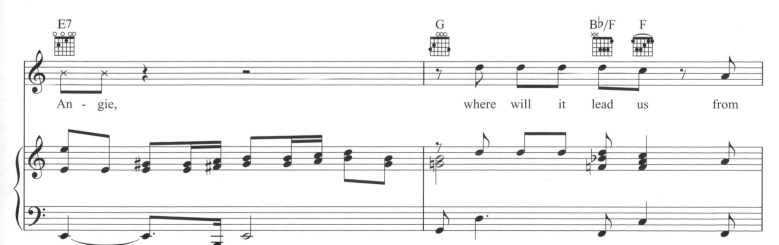

An - gie, where will it lead us from

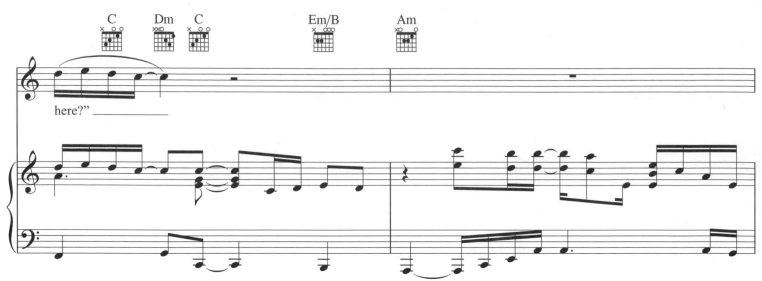

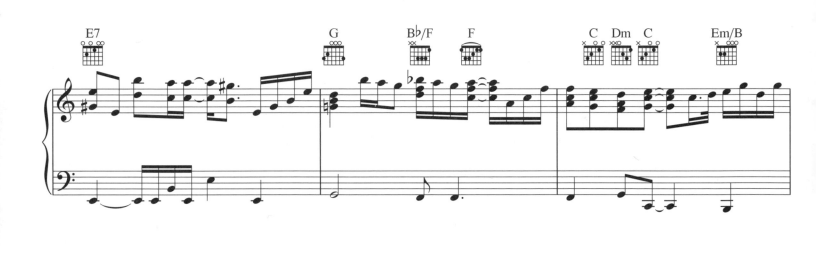

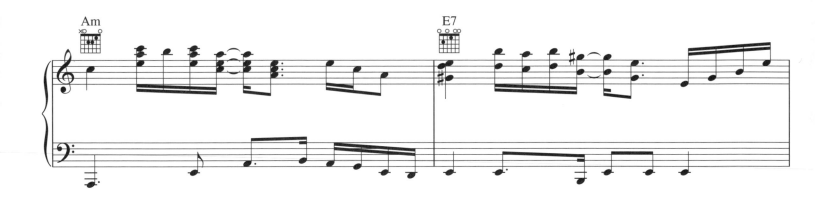

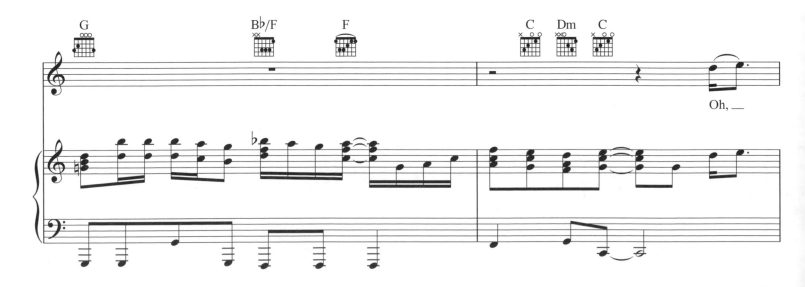

yes.

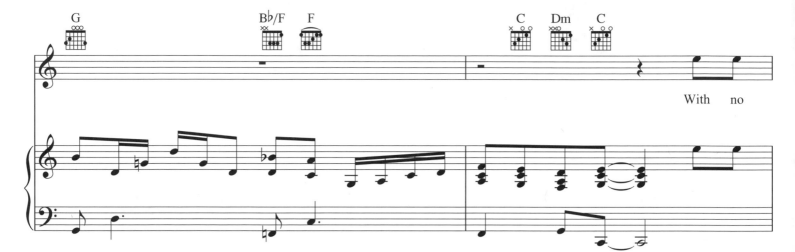

With no

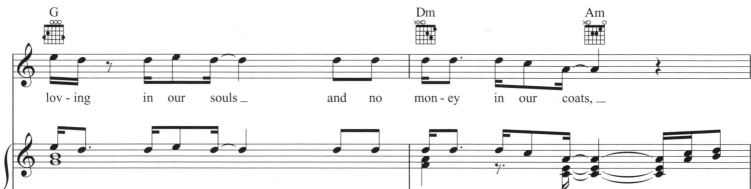

lov - ing   in our souls ___   and no   mon - ey   in our coats, ___

you can't   say ___ we're sat - is - fied, _____   but,

An - gie, I still __ love you, ba - by.

Ev -'ry - where I ___ look I see your eyes. ___

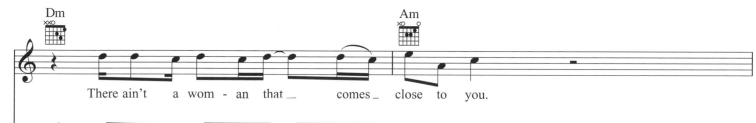

There ain't a wom - an that __ comes __ close to you.

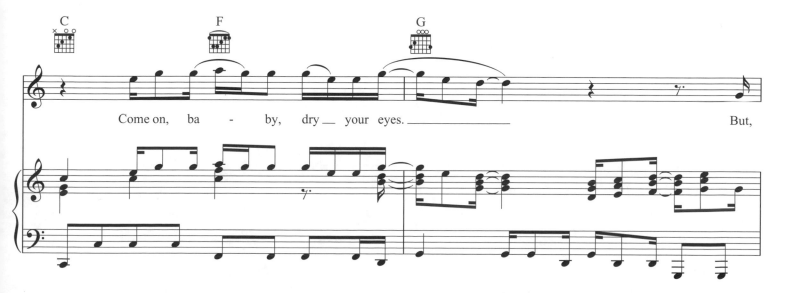

Come on, ba - by, dry __ your eyes. _____ But,

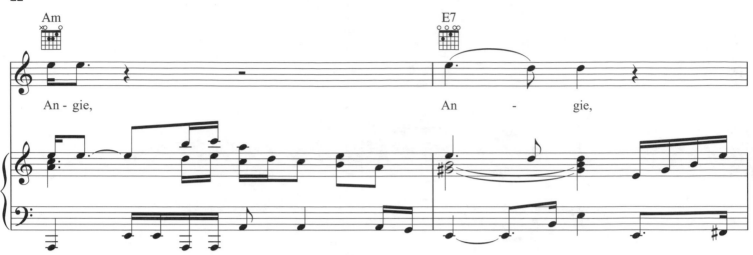

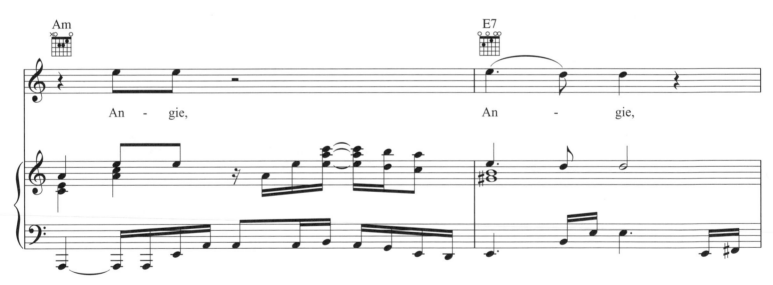

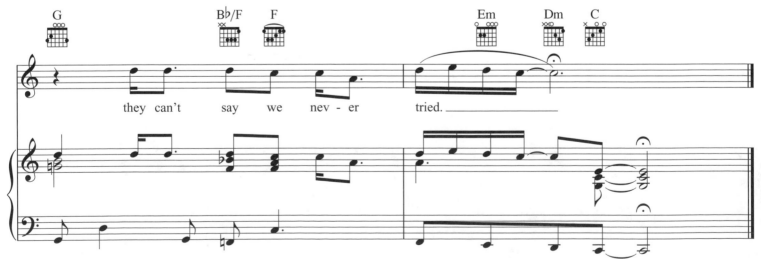

BABY, I LOVE YOUR WAY

Words and Music by
PETER FRAMPTON

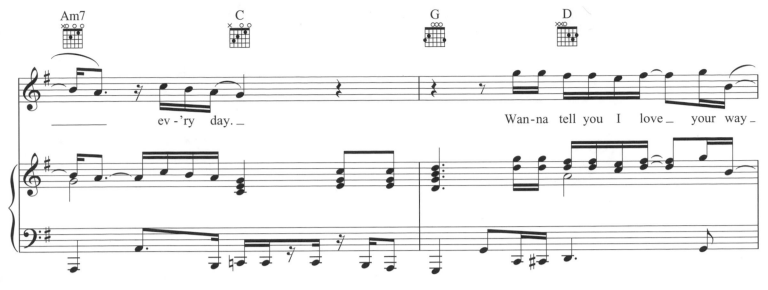

ev-'ry day. _ Wan-na tell you I love _ your way _

ev-'ry day. _ Wan-na be with you night _ and day. _

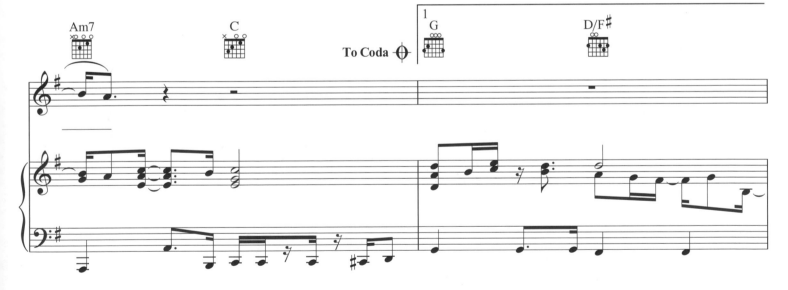

To Coda

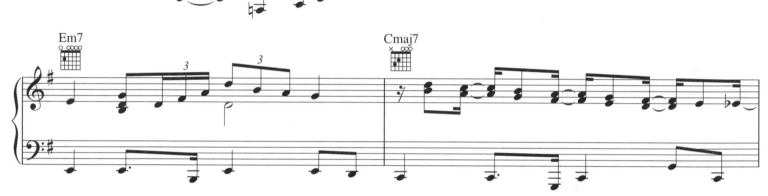

But don't hes-i-tate, ___ 'cause your

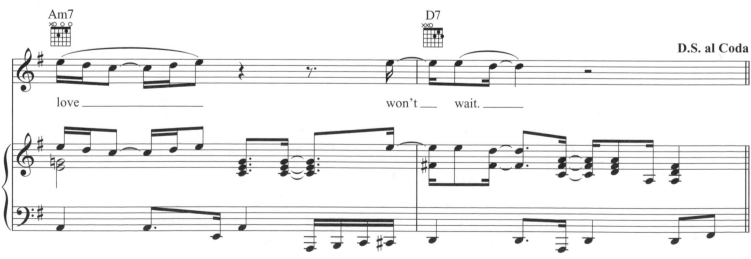

love _____ won't __ wait. _____

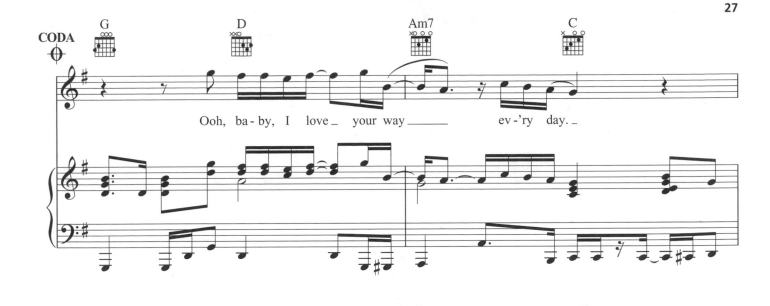

Ooh, ba - by, I love_ your way _____ ev -'ry day. _

Wan - na tell you I love_ your way. _____ Ooh. _____

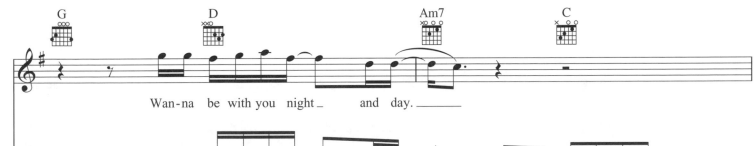

Wan - na be with you night _ and day. _____

ANNIE'S SONG

Words and Music by
JOHN DENVER

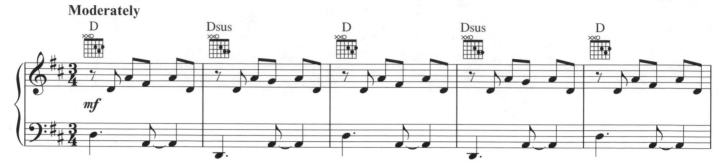

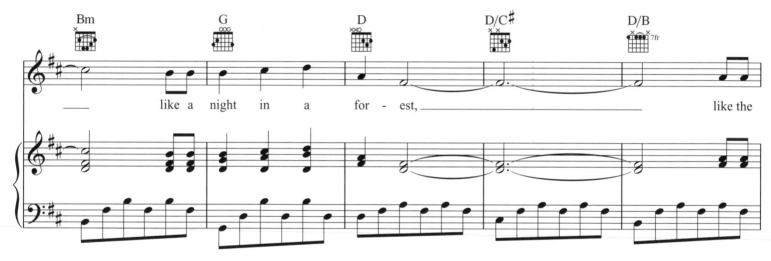

rain, _____ like a storm in the des -

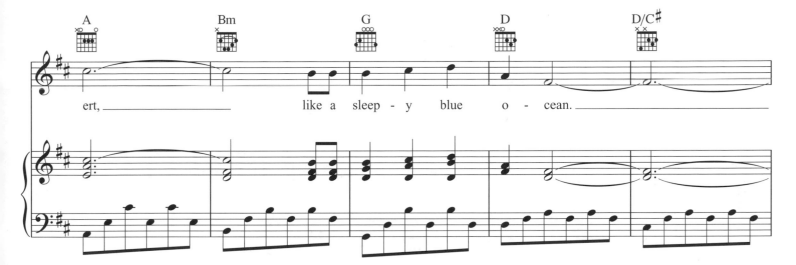

ert, _____ like a sleep - y blue o - cean. _____

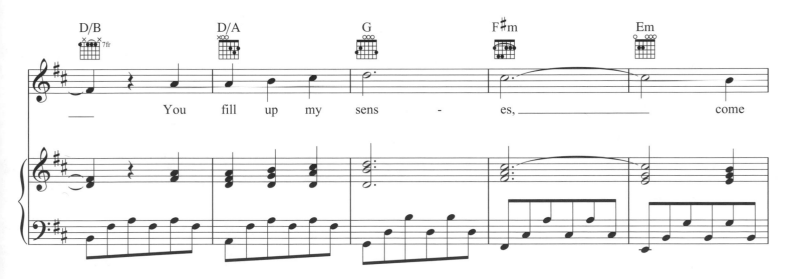

___ You fill up my sens - es, _____ come

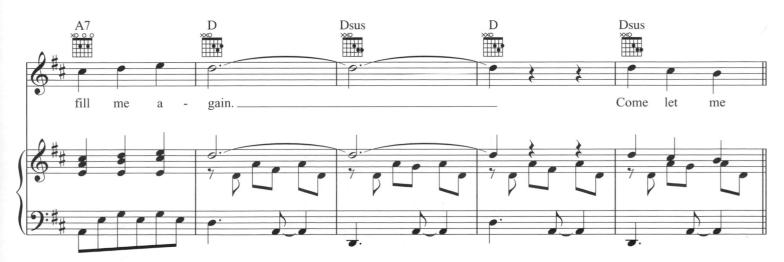

fill me a - gain. _____ Come let me

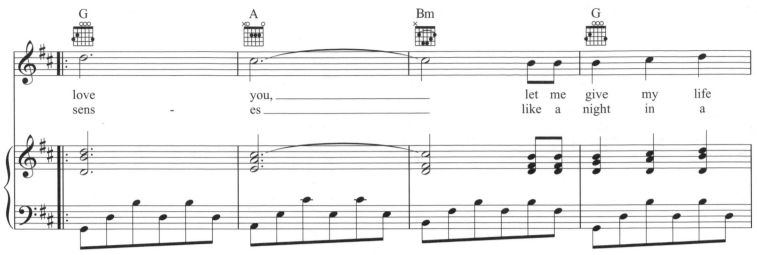

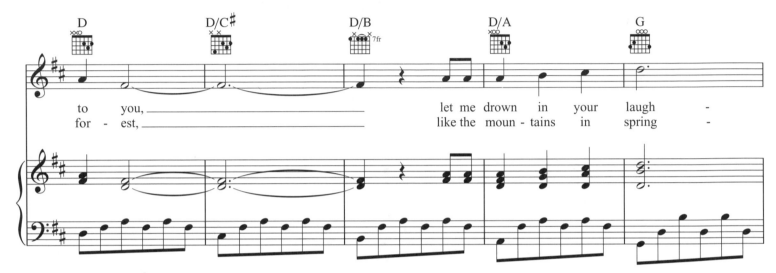

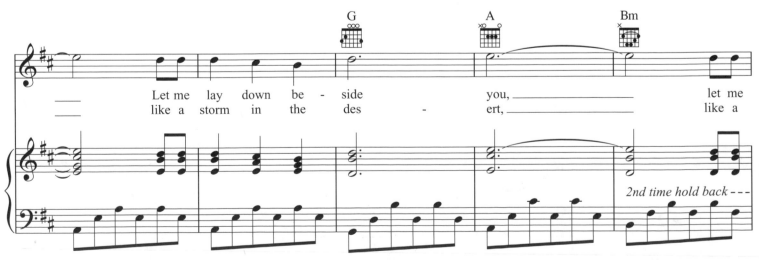

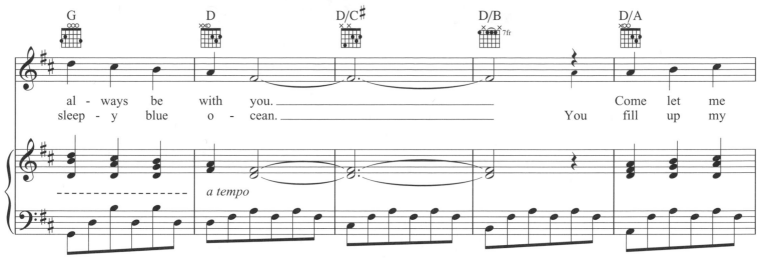

al - ways be with you. ___ Come let me
sleep - y blue o - cean. ___ You Come fill up my

a tempo

love you, ___ come love me a - gain. ___
sens - es, ___ come fill me a -

You fill up my gain. ___

dim.

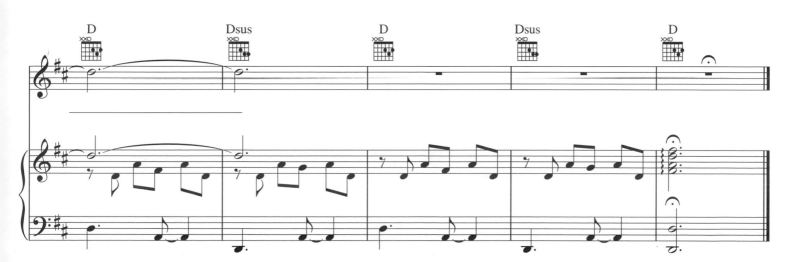

AT SEVENTEEN

Words and Music by
JANIS IAN

learned the truth at sev - en - teen, ___ that love was meant for beau -
brown - eyed girl in hand - me - downs ___ whose name I nev - er could
those of us who know ___ the pain ___ of val - en - tines that nev -

- ty queens ___ and high school girls ___ with clear - skinned smiles ___ who
___ pro - nounce ___ said, "Pit - y, please, ___ the ones ___ who serve. ___ They
- er came, ___ and those whose names ___ were nev - er called ___ when

sev - en-teen, I learned __ the truth. __ And
ha - ven for the el - der - ly." __ Re -
ug - ly duck-ling girls __ like me. __ We all

those of us __ with rav - aged fac - es, lack-ing in the so -
mem - ber those __ who win __ the game, __ lose the love they sought __
play the game __ and when __ we dare __ to cheat our-selves at sol -

- cial grac - es, des - p'rate-ly __ re - mained __ at home __ in -
__ to gain __ in de - ben - tures __ of qual - i - ty __ and
- i - taire, __ in - vent - ing lov - ers on __ the phone, __ re -

BABE, I'M GONNA LEAVE YOU

Words and Music by ANNE BREDON,
JIMMY PAGE and ROBERT PLANT

Moderately slow

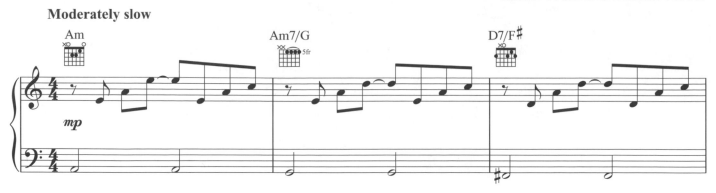

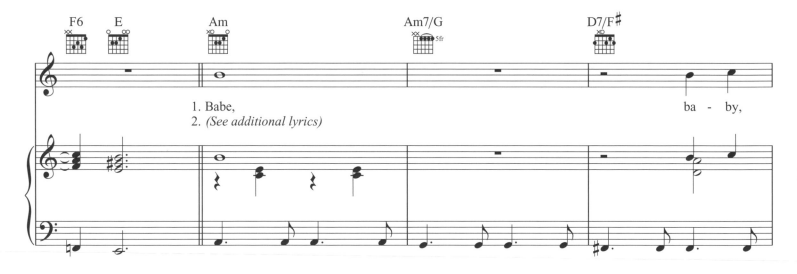

1. Babe,
2. *(See additional lyrics)*

ba - by,

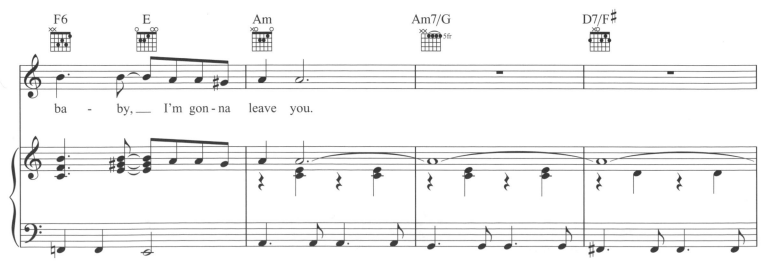

ba - by, __ I'm gon - na leave you.

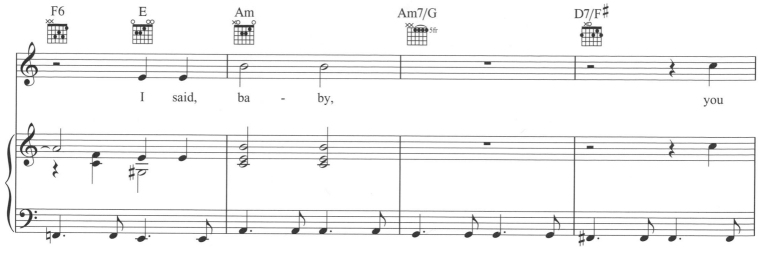

I said, ba - by, you

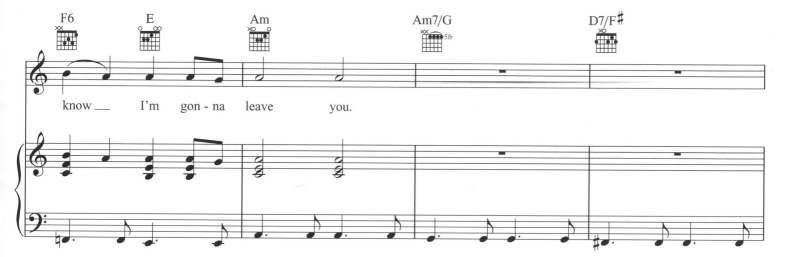

know __ I'm gon - na leave you.

I'll leave you when the sum - mer - time, __ leave you when the

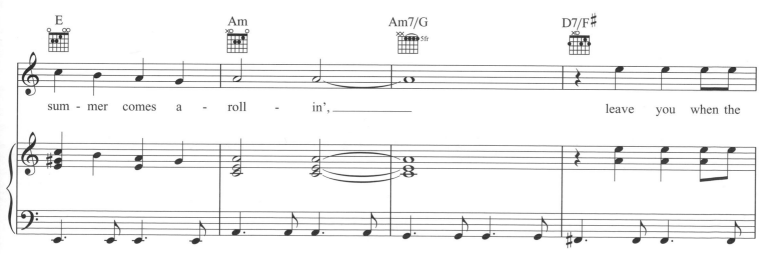

sum - mer comes a - roll - in', __ leave you when the

sum - mer comes a - long. ____

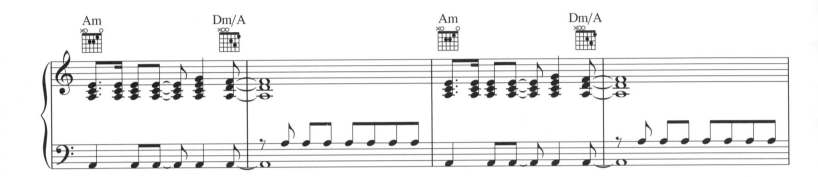

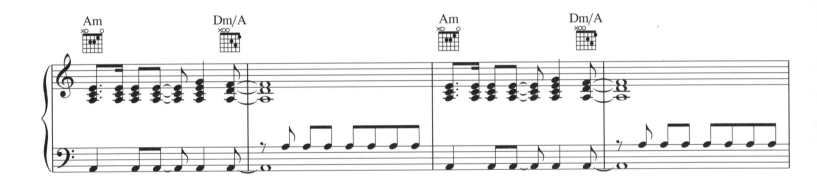

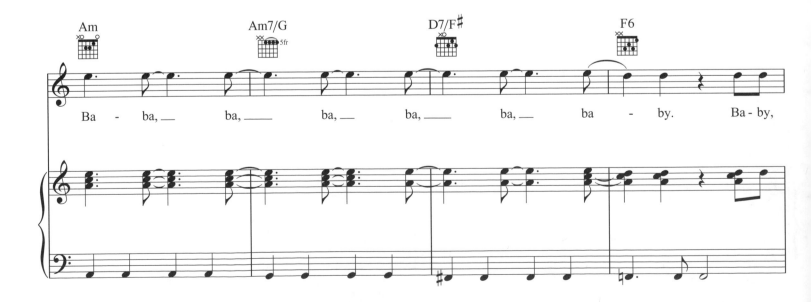

Ba - ba, ____ ba, ____ ba, ____ ba, ____ ba, ____ ba - by. Ba - by,

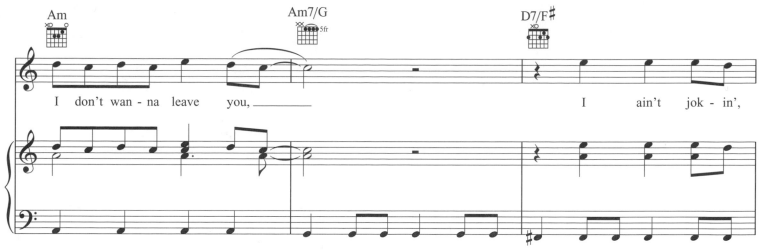

I don't wan-na leave you, ___ I ain't jok-in',

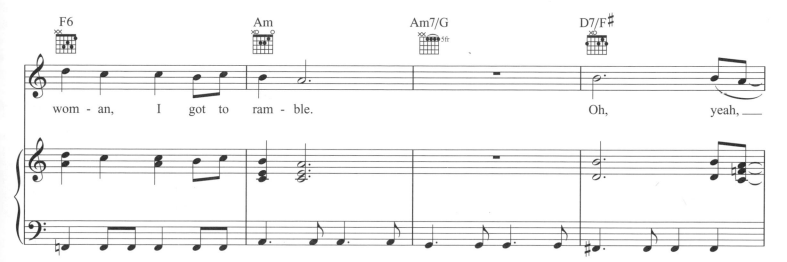

wom-an, I got to ram-ble. Oh, yeah, ___

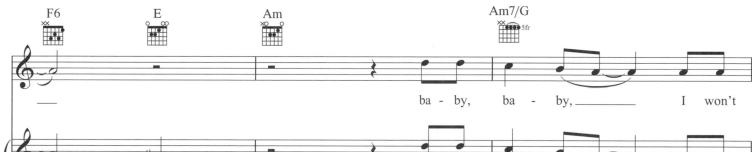

ba - by, ba - by, ___ I won't

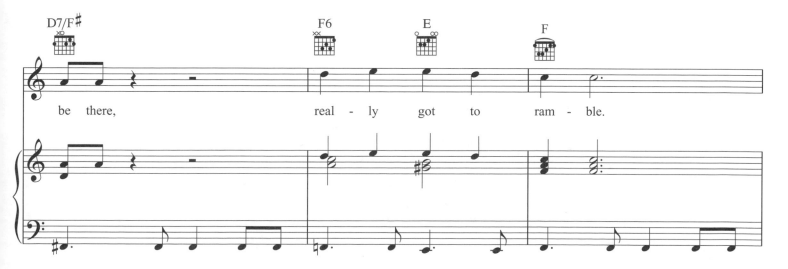

be there, real - ly got to ram-ble.

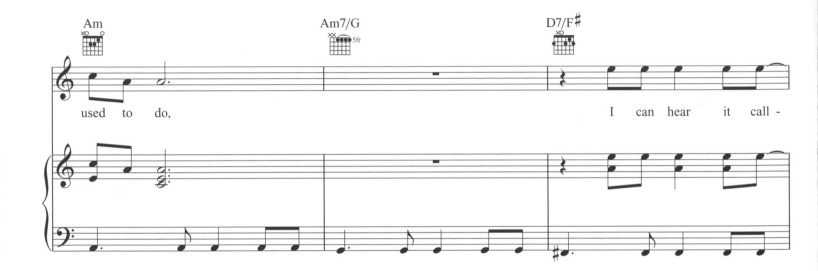

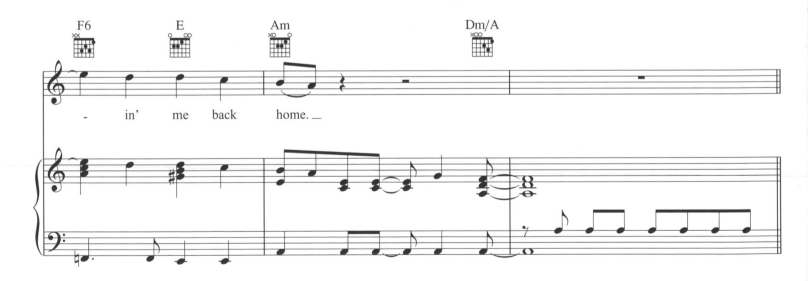

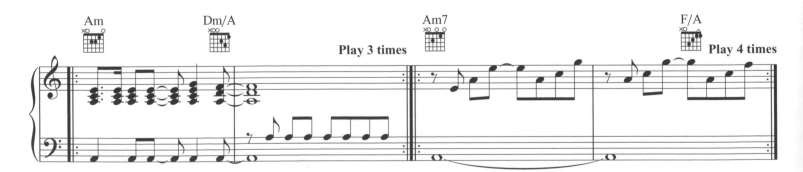

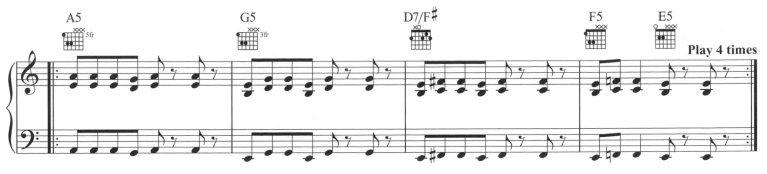

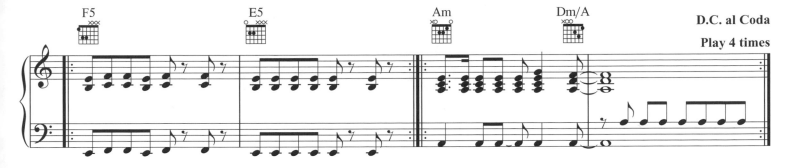

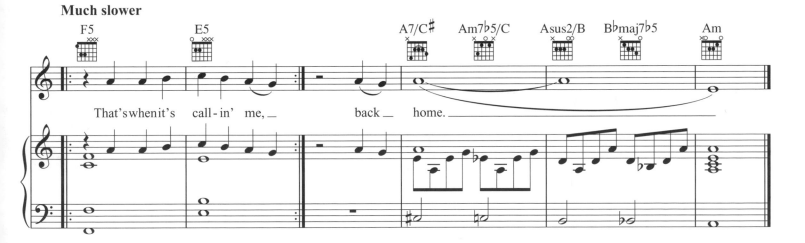

Additional Lyrics

2. I know, I know, I know, I never, I never, I never, I never, I never leave you, baby
   But I got to go away from this place, I've got to quit you.
   Ooh, baby, baby, baby, baby
   Baby, baby, baby, ooh don't you hear it callin'?
   Woman, woman, I know, I know it's good to have you back again
   And I know that one day, baby, it's really gonna grow, yes it is.
   We gonna go walkin' through the park every day.
   Hear what I say, every day.
   Baby, it's really growin', you made me happy when skies were grey.
   But now I've got to go away
   Baby, baby, baby, baby
   That's when it's callin' me
   That's when it's callin' me back home...

BAND ON THE RUN

Words and Music by PAUL McCARTNEY
and LINDA McCARTNEY

Moderately

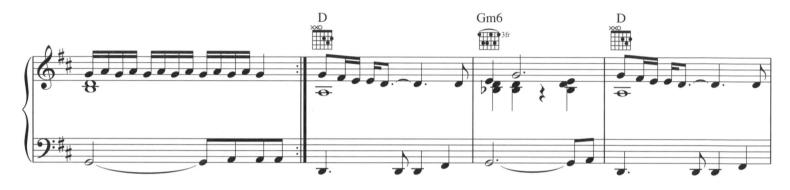

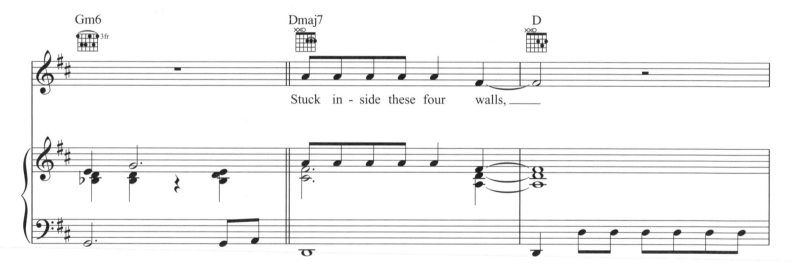

Stuck in-side these four walls, _____

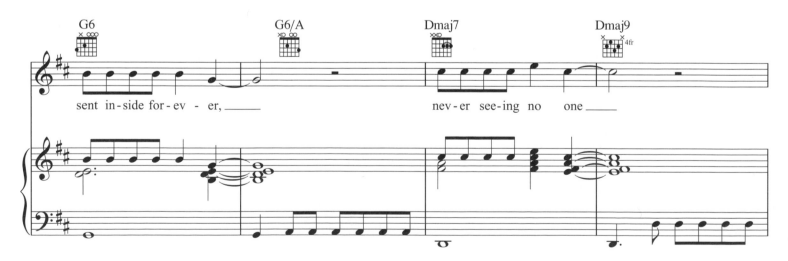

sent in-side for-ev - er, _____ nev-er see-ing no one _____

nice a - gain _____ like you, _____ ma - ma,

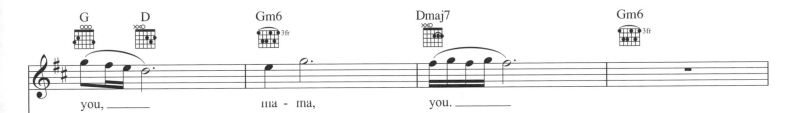

you, _____ ma - ma, you. _____

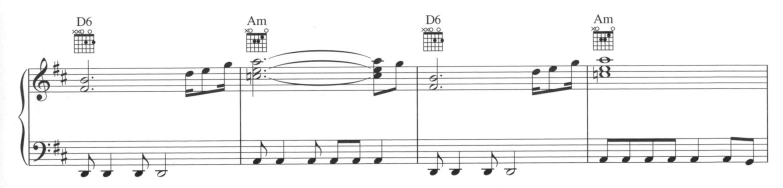

If I ev-er get out __ of here   thought of giv-ing it all __ a-way   to a reg-is-tered char - i - ty.

All I need is a pint __ a day if I   ev-er get out __ of here, __   (if we ev-er get out __ of here.) __

Faster

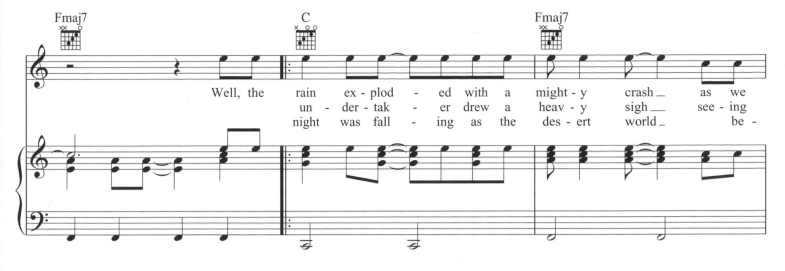

Well, the rain ex- plod- ed with a might-y crash___ as we
un- der- tak- er drew a heav-y sigh___ see- ing
night was fall- ing as the des- ert world___ be-

fell in- to ___ the sun, ___ and the first one said to the
no one else ___ had come, ___ and a bell was ring- ing in the
gan to set - tle down. ___ In the town they're search-ing for us

sec- ond one there ___ I hope you're hav- ing fun. ___
vil - lage square ___ for the rab - bits on the run. ___
ev - 'ry - where ___ but we nev- er will be found. ___

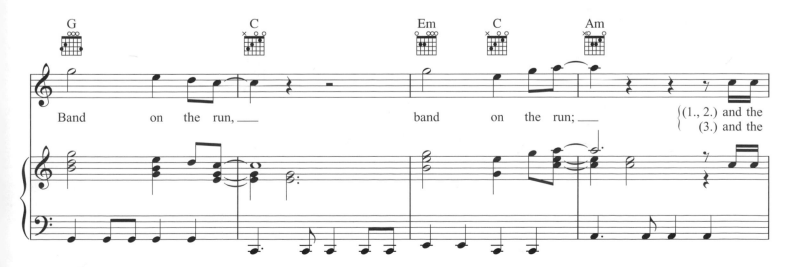

Band on the run, ___ band on the run; ___ ((1., 2.) and the
(3.) and the

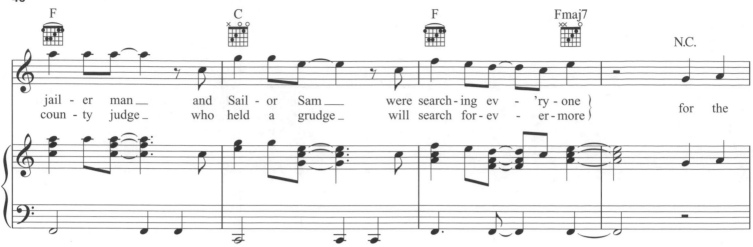

jail - er man ___ and Sail - or Sam ___ were search-ing ev - 'ry-one
coun - ty judge ___ who held a grudge ___ will search for-ev - er-more

for the

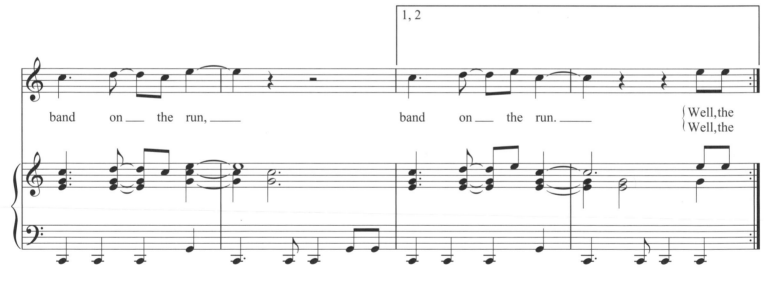

band   on ___ the run, _____   band   on ___ the run, _____

band   on ___ the run, _____   band   on ___ the run. _____

1, 2

band   on ___ the run, _____   band   on ___ the run. _____

{ Well, the
{ Well, the

3

band   on ___ the run. _____

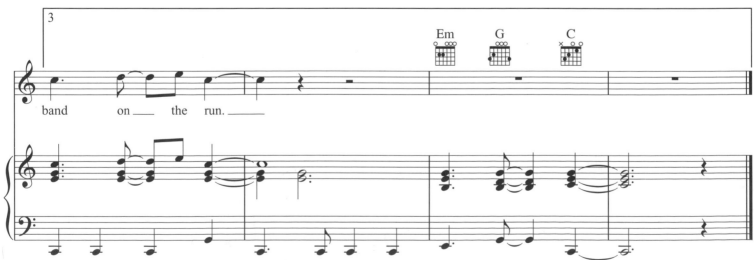

BEHIND BLUE EYES

Words and Music by
PETE TOWNSHEND

Moderately

Esus

Em   G   D

No one knows _ what it's like _ to be the bad _ man,
No one knows _ what it's like _ to feel these feel - ings

C6/9

to be the sad _ man   be - hind _
like I do, _   and I _

A(add2)   Em

_ blue eyes. _   No one knows _ what it's like _
_ blame you. _   No one bites _ back as hard _

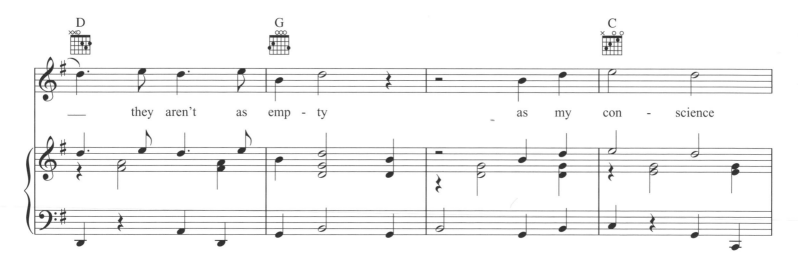

on - ly lone - ly. _____ My love is ven - geance _____

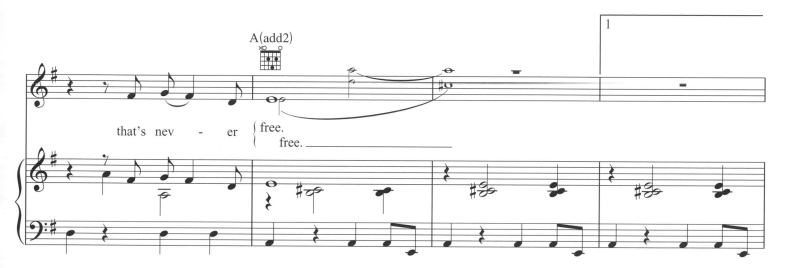

that's nev - er { free.
{ free. _____

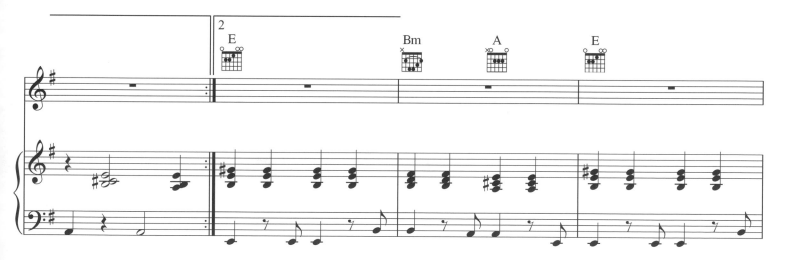

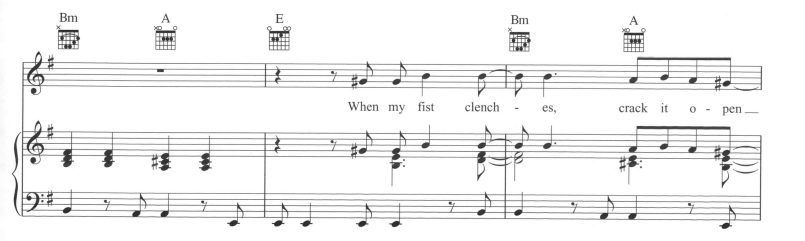

When my fist clench - es, crack it o - pen _____

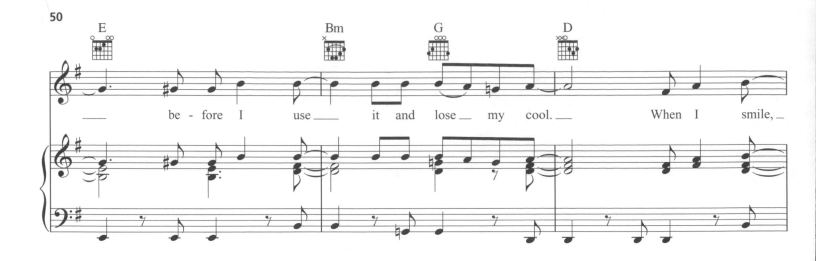

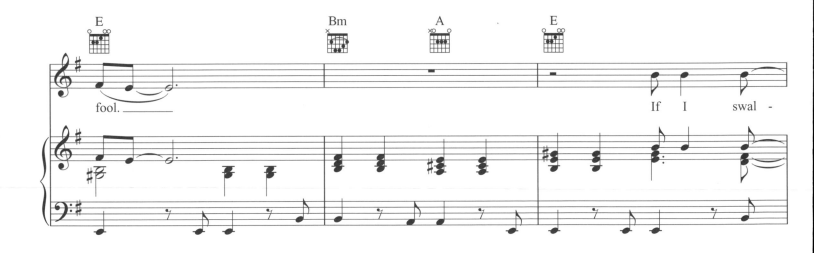

throat. And if I shiv - er, please give me a blan - ket. Keep me warm; ___

___ let me wear your coat. ___ No one knows ___ what it's like ___

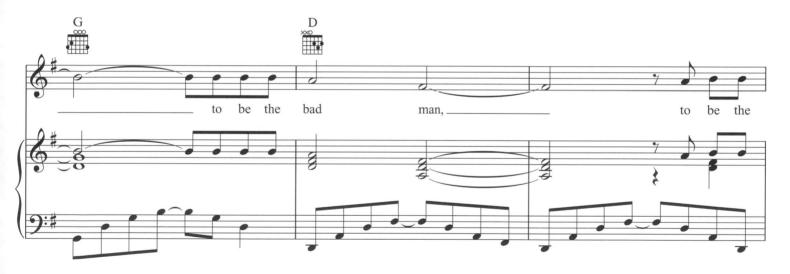

___ to be the bad man, _____ to be the

sad man be - hind ___ blue eyes. _____

BLACKBIRD

Words and Music by JOHN LENNON
and PAUL McCARTNEY

Slowly and smoothly

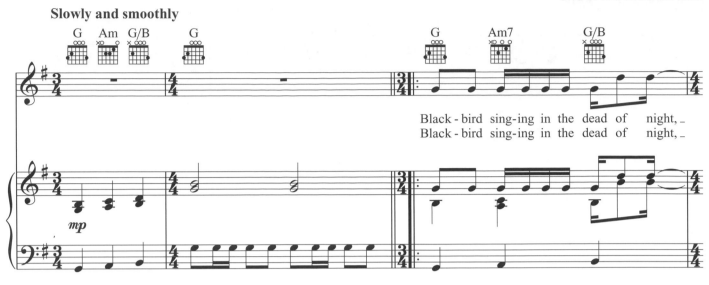

Black-bird sing-ing in the dead of night, _
Black-bird sing-ing in the dead of night, _

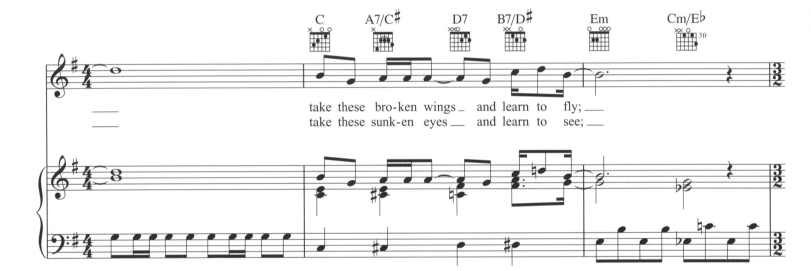

take these bro-ken wings _ and learn to fly; _
take these sunk-en eyes _ and learn to see; _

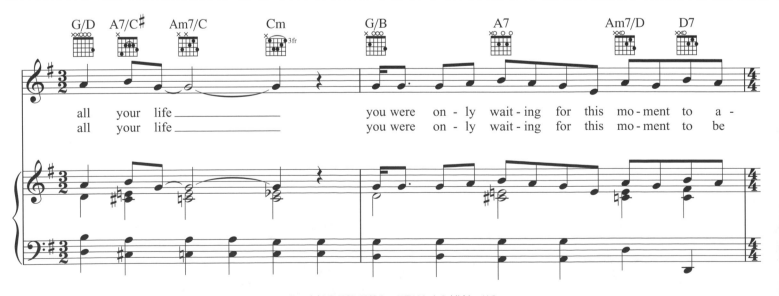

all your life _____ you were on-ly wait-ing for this mo-ment to a-
all your life _____ you were on-ly wait-ing for this mo-ment to be

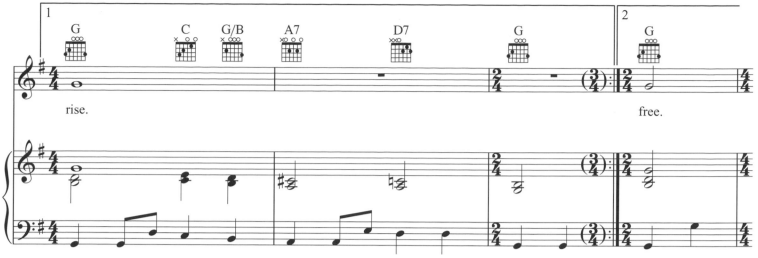

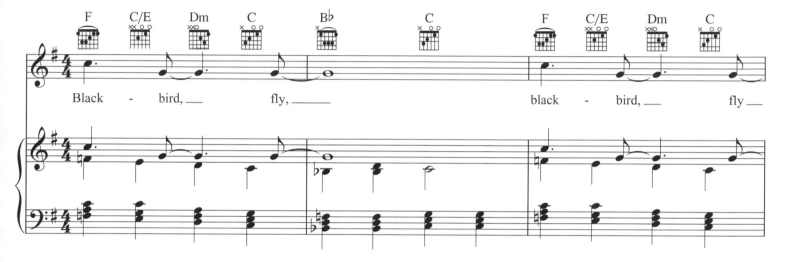

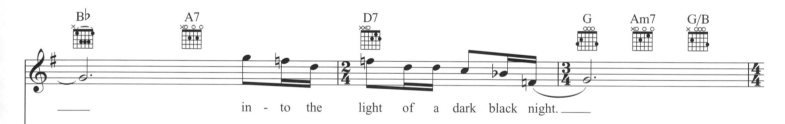

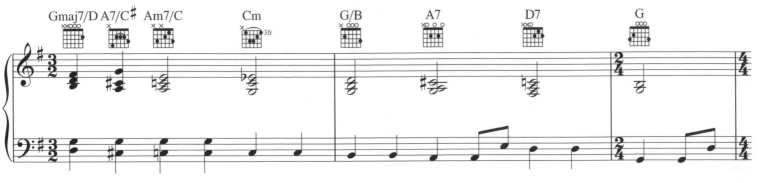

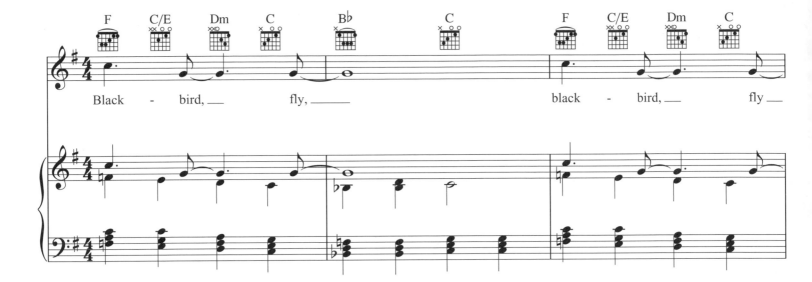

Black- bird, ___ fly, _____ black- bird, ___ fly ___

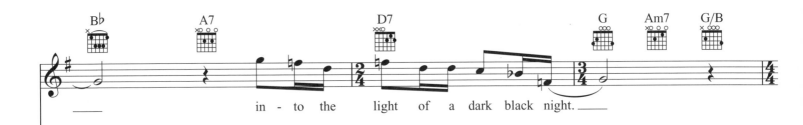

in - to the light of a dark black night. ___

molto rit.   *a tempo*

CAROLINA IN MY MIND

Words and Music by
JAMES TAYLOR

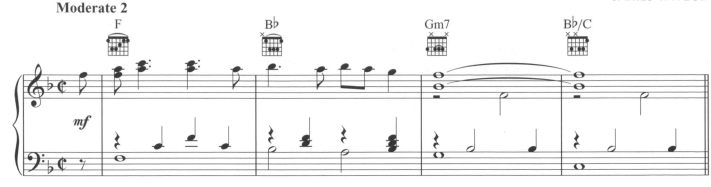

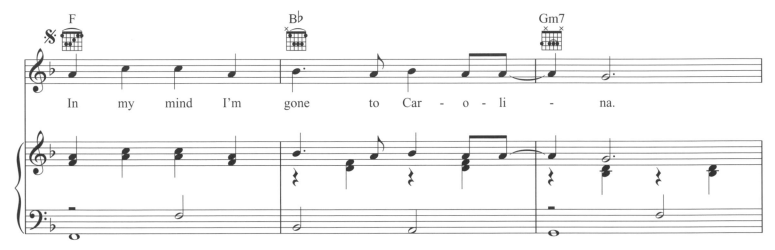

In my mind I'm gone to Car - o - li - na.

Can't you see the sun - shine? And

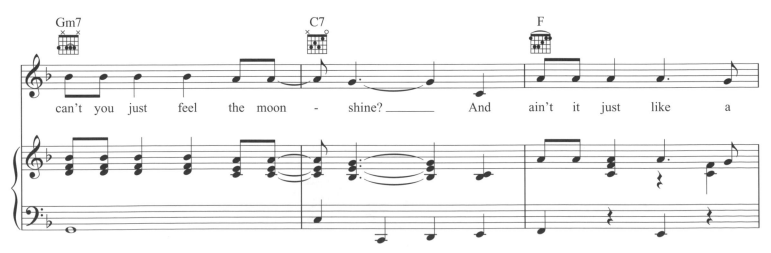

can't you just feel the moon - shine? _____ And ain't it just like a

friend of mine ___ to hit me from ___ be - hind? ___ Yes, I'm

gone to Car - o - li - na in ___ my mind. ___

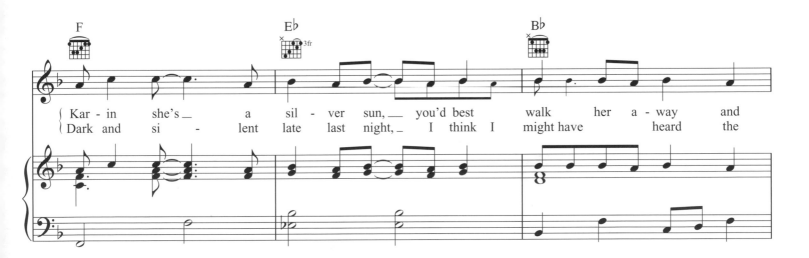

Kar - in she's ___ a sil - ver sun, ___ you'd best walk her a - way and
Dark and si - lent late last night, ___ I think I might have heard the

watch it shine. Watch her watch _____ the morn - ing come. ___
high - way call - ing, geese in flight ___ and ___ dogs that bite. ___

A sil - ver tear ___ ap - pear - ing, now I'm cry - ing,
And signs that might _ be o - mens say I'm go - ing,

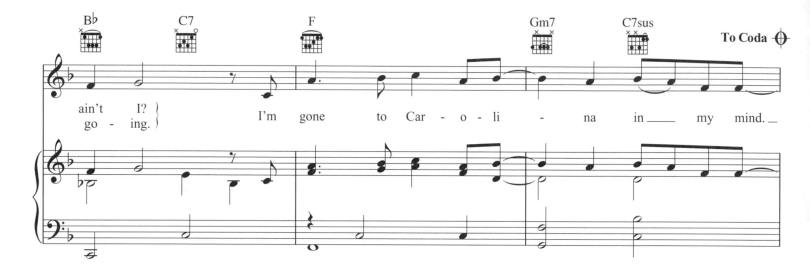

ain't I? }
go - ing. } I'm gone to Car - o - li - na in ___ my mind. _

_____ There ain't no doubt in no ___ one's mind _ that love's _

___ the fin - est thing ___ a - round, _ whis - per some -

thing soft __ and kind. And hey, babe, the

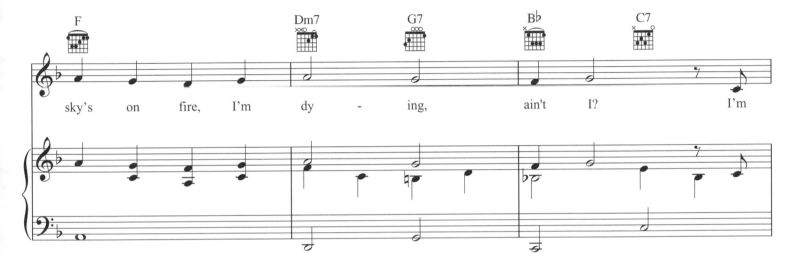

sky's on fire, I'm dy - ing, ain't I? I'm

gone to Car - o - li - na in __ my mind. _____

D.S. al Coda

CODA

_____ Now with a ho - ly host of

oth - ers stand - ing 'round ____ me, ____ no, ____

still I'm on ____ the dark side of ____ the moon. ____ And it

seems like it goes on like this for - ev - er.

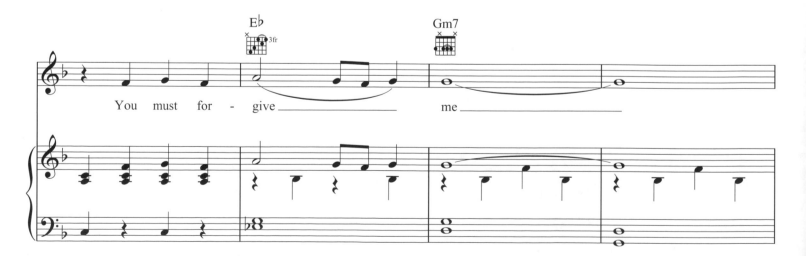

You must for - give ____ me ____

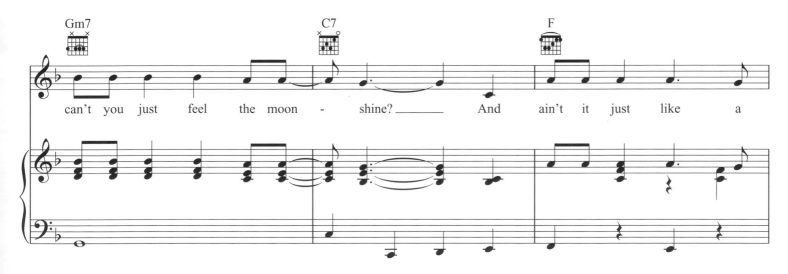

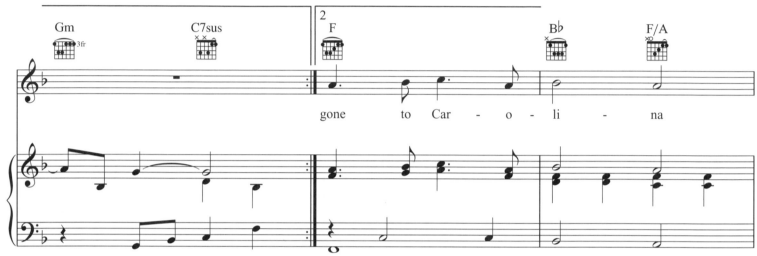

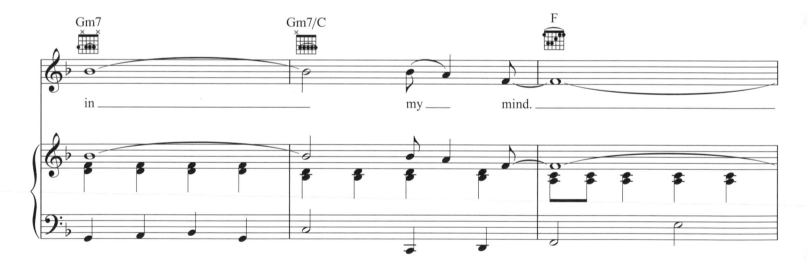

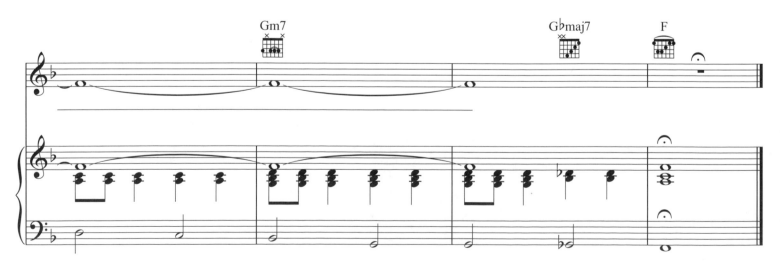

COME MONDAY

Words and Music by
JIMMY BUFFETT

And, hon - ey, I did - n't know _ that I'd be miss -
And, dar - lin', it's I love you so, _ that's the rea - son I just _
Cal - i - for - nia has worn me quite thin; _ I just can't wait to see _

- in' you so. _
_ let you go. _ } Come Mon - day _ it - 'll be all right. _ Come
_ you a - gain.

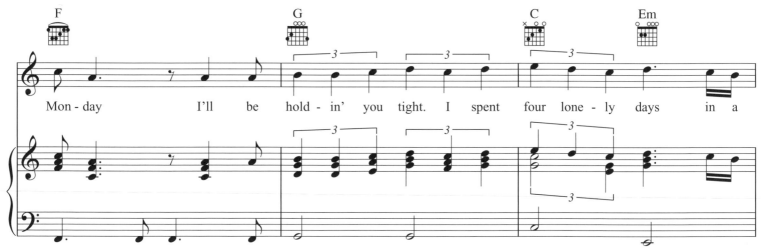

Mon - day I'll be hold - in' you tight. I spent four lone - ly days in a

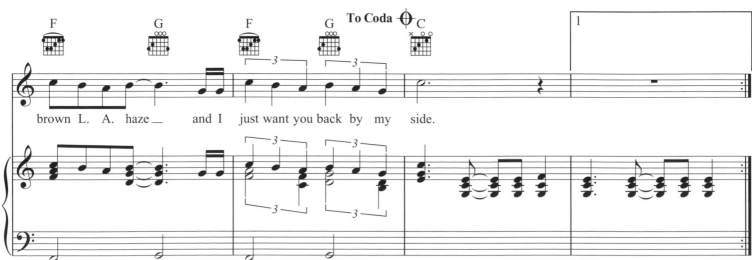

brown L. A. haze _ and I just want you back by my side.

CATCH THE WIND

Words and Music by
DONOVAN LEITCH

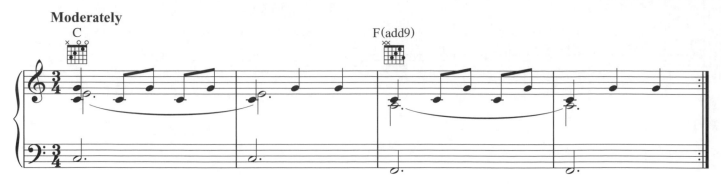

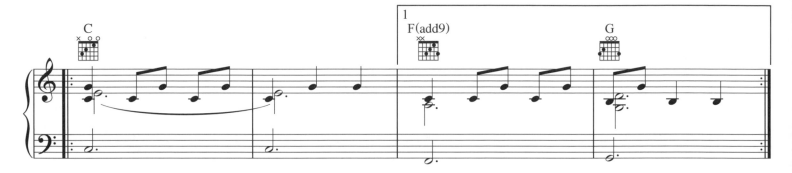

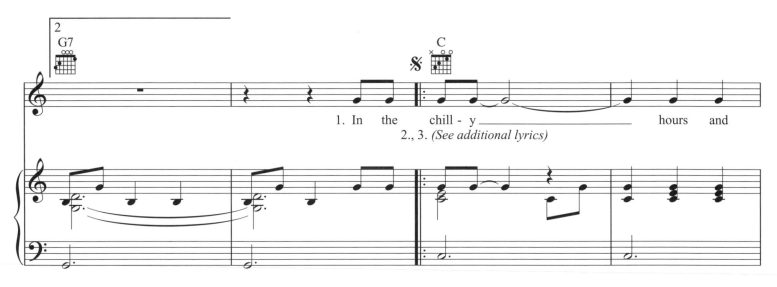

1. In the chill - y _____ hours and

2., 3. *(See additional lyrics)*

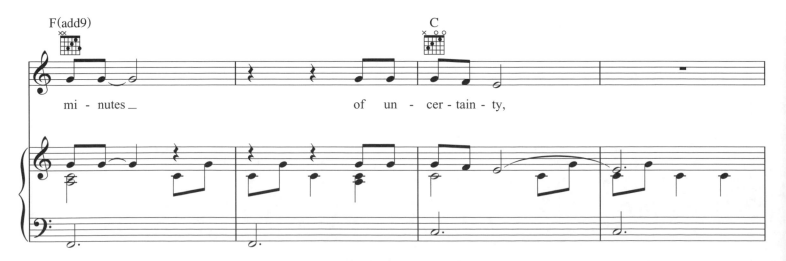

mi - nutes ___ of un - cer - tain - ty,

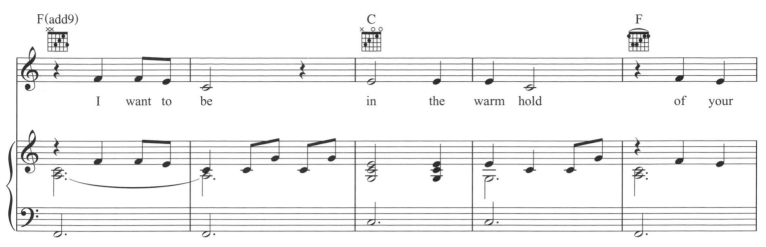

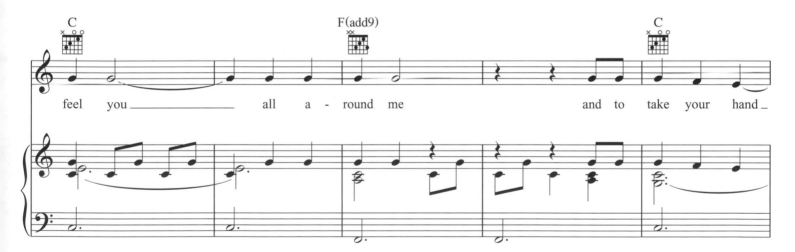

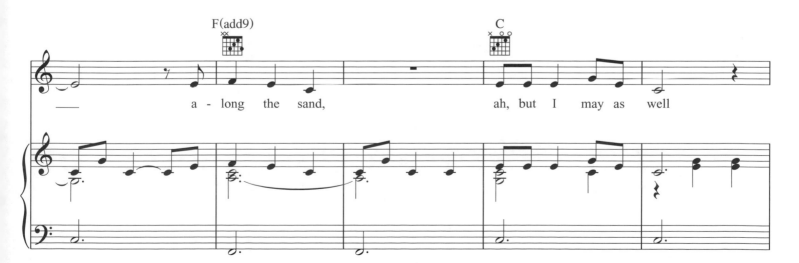

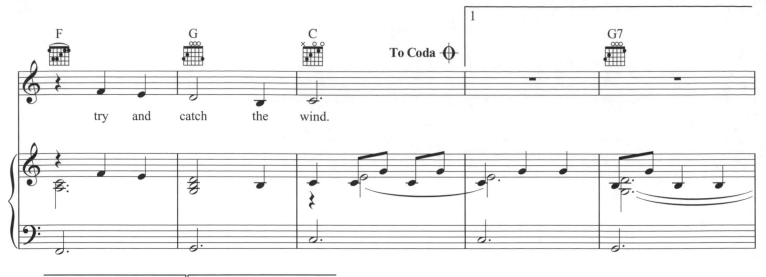

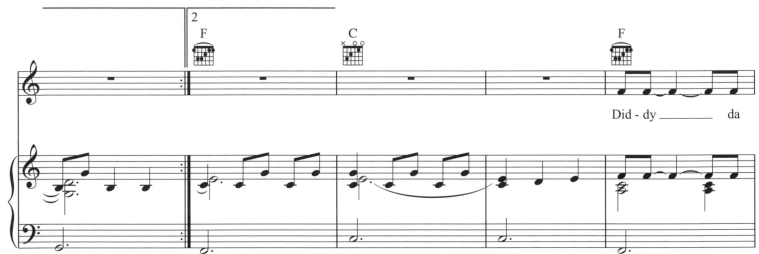

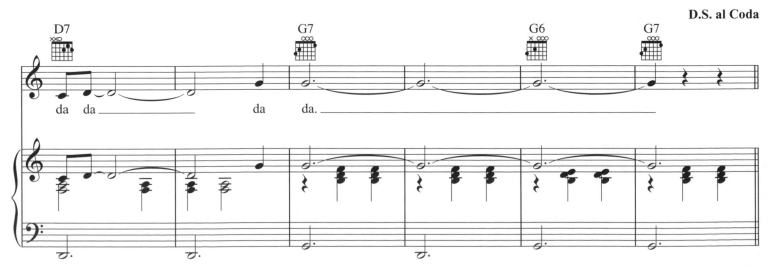

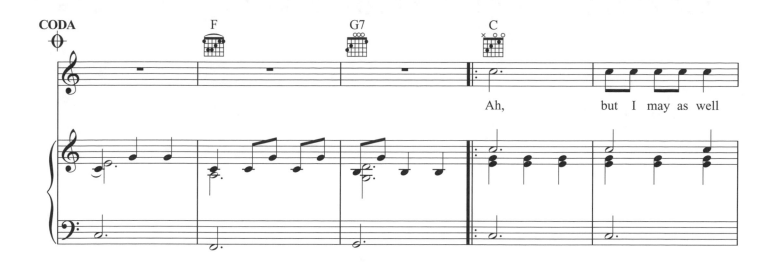

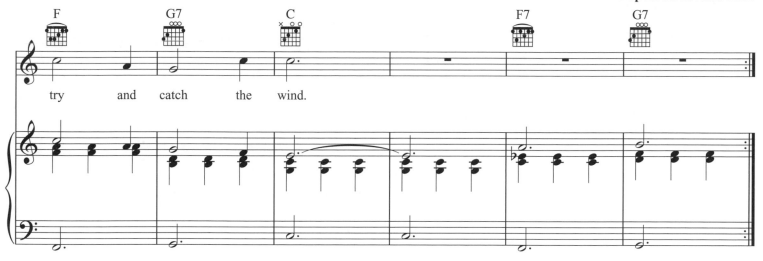

Additional Lyrics

2. When sundown pales the sky
   I want to hide awhile
   Behind your smile
   And everywhere I'd look, your eyes I'd find.
   For me to love you now
   Would be the sweetest thing
   'Twould make me sing
   Ah, but I may as well try and catch the wind.

3. When rain has hung the leaves with tears
   I want you near
   To kill my fears
   To help me leave all my blues behind
   For standing in your heart
   Is where I want to be
   And I long to be
   Ah, but I may as well try and catch the wind.

CRAZY LITTLE THING CALLED LOVE

Words and Music by
FREDDIE MERCURY

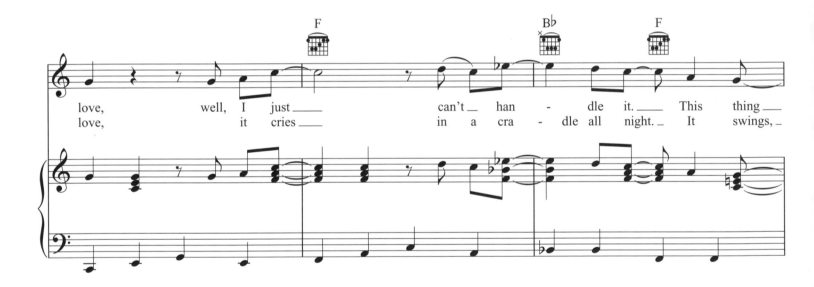

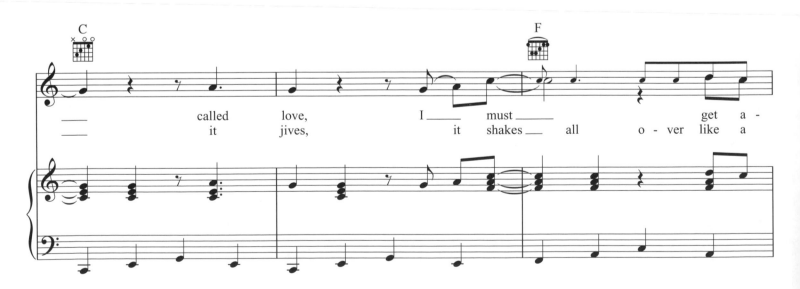

round to it. ___ I ain't ___ read - y.
jel - ly - fish. ___ I kind - a like it.
Cra - zy lit - tle thing called

love.
1 Well, this thing ___
2 There goes my ba - by; ___

she knows ___ how to rock and roll. ___ She drives ___ me

cra - zy. ___ She gives me hot and cold fe - ver. She

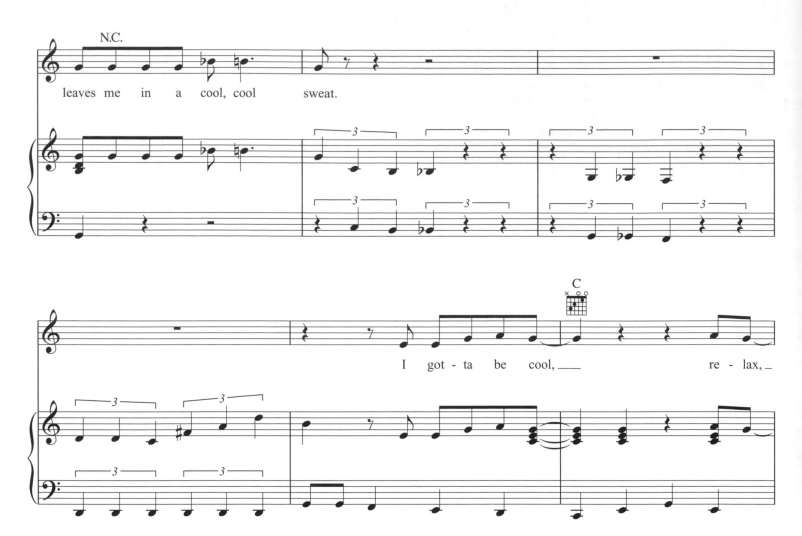

leaves me in a cool, cool sweat.

I got - ta be cool, ___ re - lax, ___

___ a - get hip, ___ a - get on my tracks. Take a

back seat, hitch - hike ___ and take a long ride ___ on a

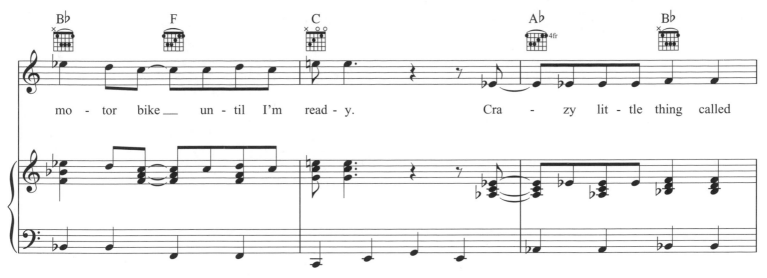

mo - tor bike __ un - til I'm read - y. Cra - zy lit - tle thing called

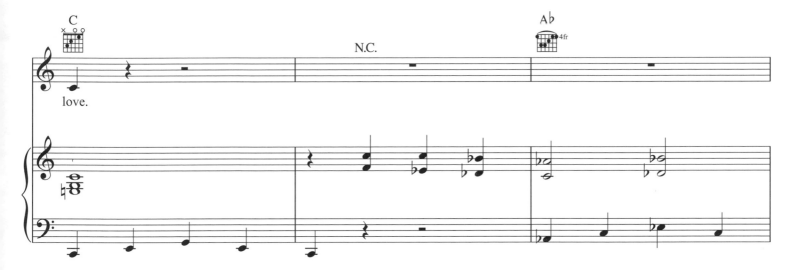

love.

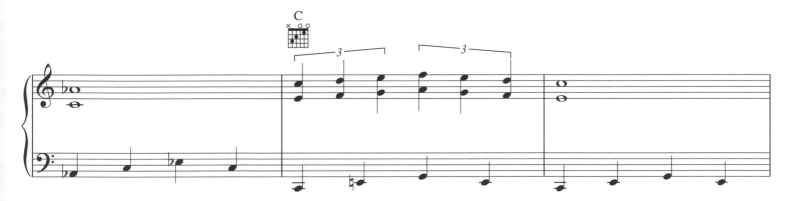

74

I got - ta be cool, ___ re - lax, _

___ a - get hip, ___ a - get on my tracks. Take a

back seat, ___ hitch - hike ___ to take a lit - tle long_ ride_ on my

mo - tor bike ___ un - til I'm read - y. Cra - zy lit - tle thing called

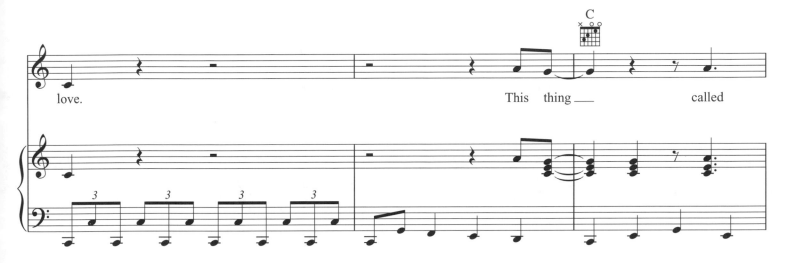

love. This thing ___ called

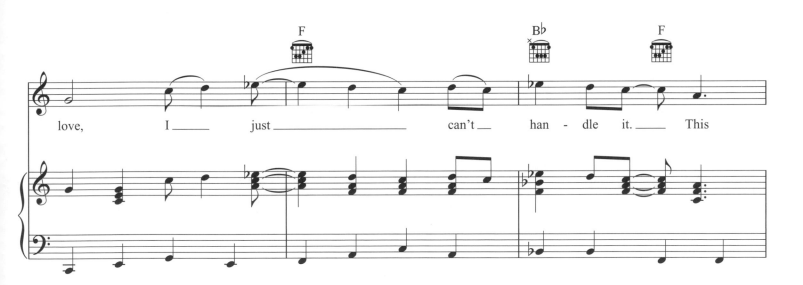

love, I ___ just _____ can't ___ han - dle it. ___ This

thing called love, I ___ must ___ get a -

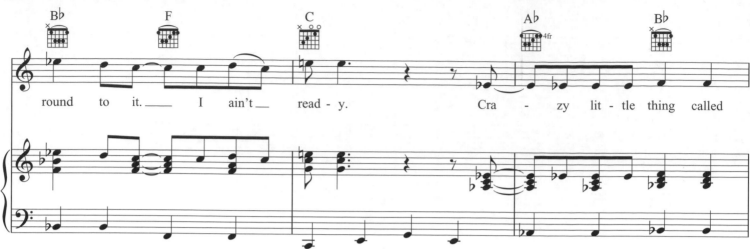

round to it. ___ I ain't ___ read - y. Cra - zy lit - tle thing called

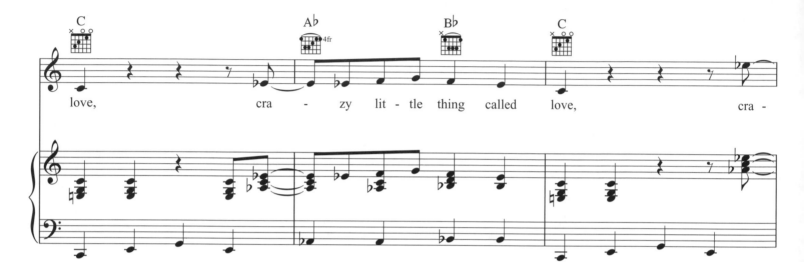

love, cra - zy lit - tle thing called love, cra -

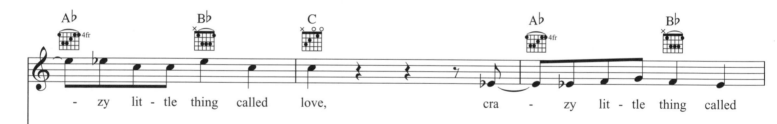

- zy lit - tle thing called love, cra - zy lit - tle thing called

love, hey, cra - zy lit - tle thing called love.

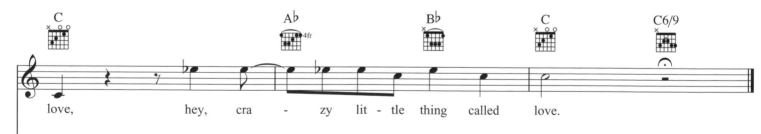

GIVE A LITTLE BIT

Words and Music by RICK DAVIES
and ROGER HODGSON

Give a lit-tle bit,

give a lit-tle bit ___ of your love ___ to me.

I'll give a lit-tle bit, ___ I'll give a lit-tle bit ___ of my { love ___ / life ___ }

There's so much that we need
Now's the time that we need

to share, so send a smile and show you care.
to share, so

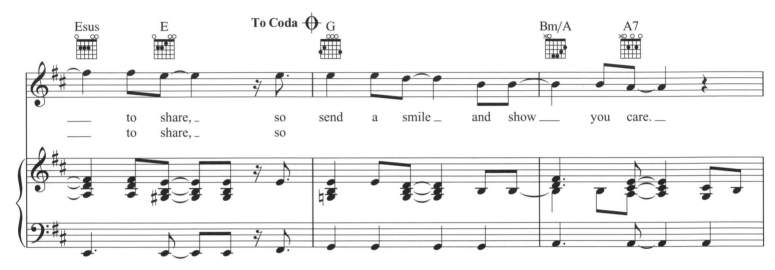

I'll give a lit-tle bit,

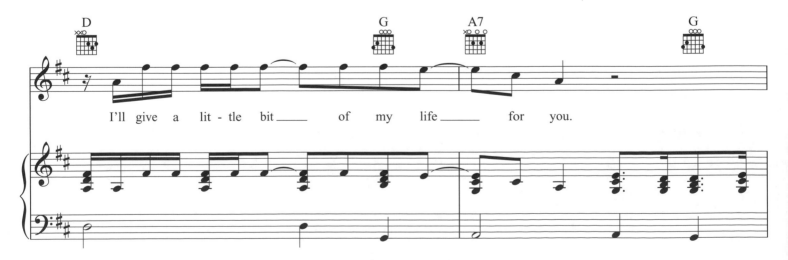

I'll give a lit-tle bit of my life for you.

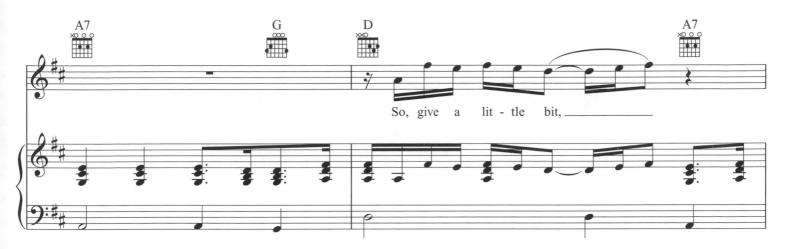

So, give a lit-tle bit, _____

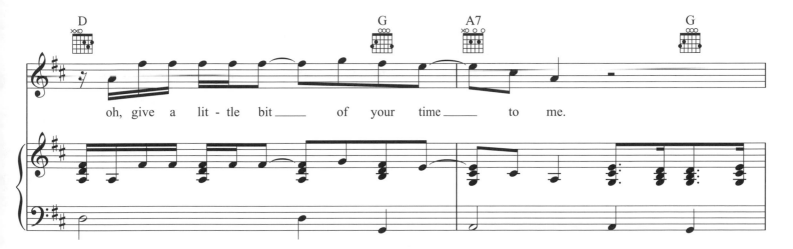

oh, give a lit-tle bit _____ of your time _____ to me.

See the man _____ with the lone - ly eyes? _____ Oh,

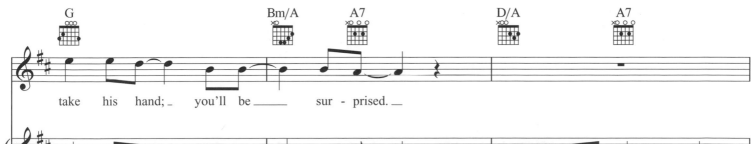

take his hand; _____ you'll be _____ sur - prised. _____

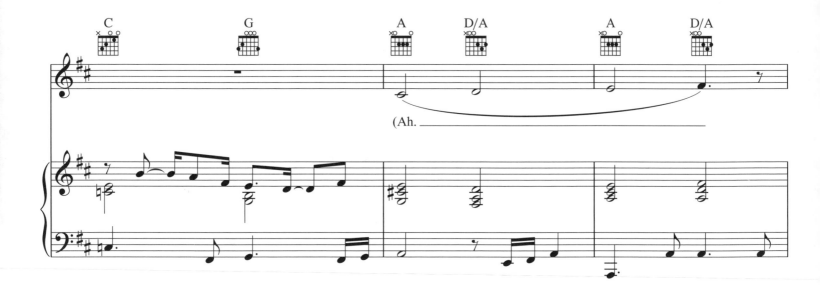

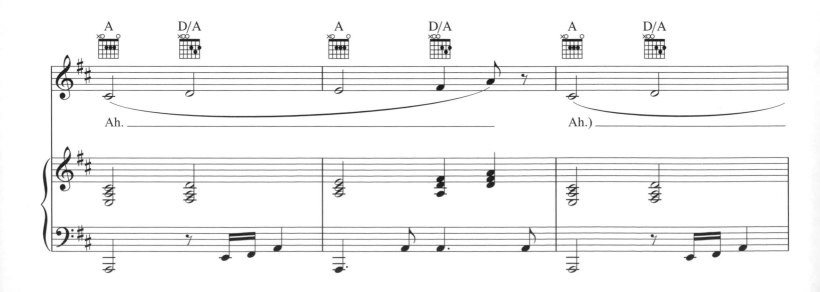

DUST IN THE WIND

Words and Music by
KERRY LIVGREN

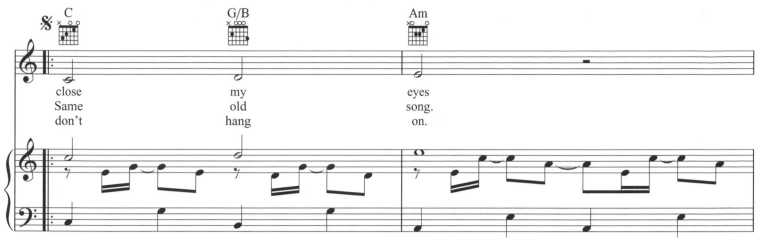

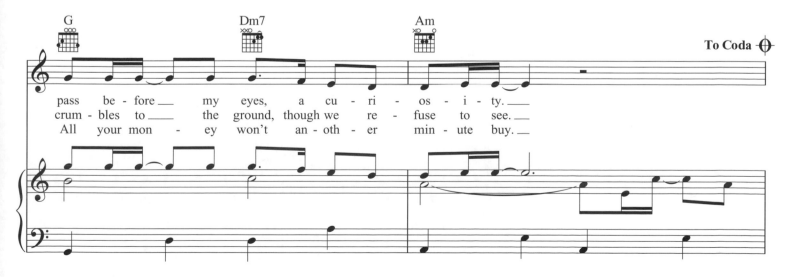

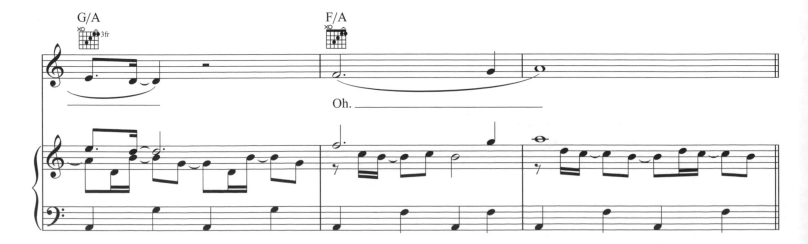

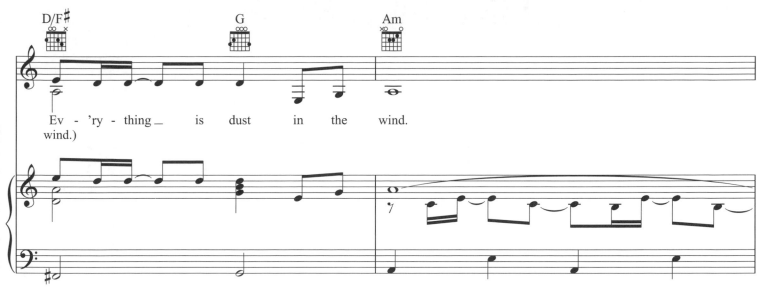

Ev - 'ry - thing __ is dust in the wind.
wind.)

Repeat and Fade

Optional Ending

poco rit.

FIRE AND RAIN

Words and Music by
JAMES TAYLOR

Slowly

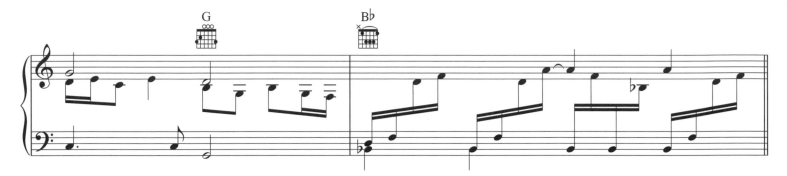

Just yes-ter-day morn-ing they let me know __ you were gone. __
look down up-on me, Je-sus? You got-ta help me make a stand.

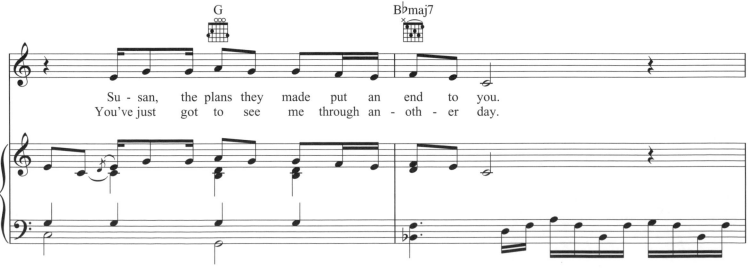

Su-san, the plans they made put an end to you.
You've just got to see me through an-oth-er day.

I walked out this morn - ing and I wrote down this song. __
My bod - y's ach - ing and my time is at hand __

I just can't re - mem - ber who to send __ it to. __
and I __ won't make it an - y oth - er way. __

I've seen fire and I've seen rain. I've seen

sun - ny days _ that I thought _ would nev - er end. _ I've seen

lone - ly times _ when I could not find a friend, _ but I

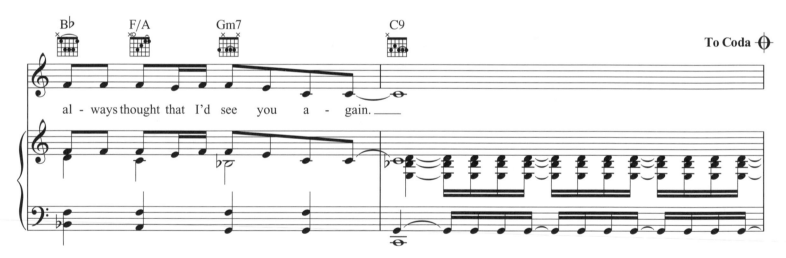

al - ways thought that I'd see you a - gain. _

To Coda ⊕

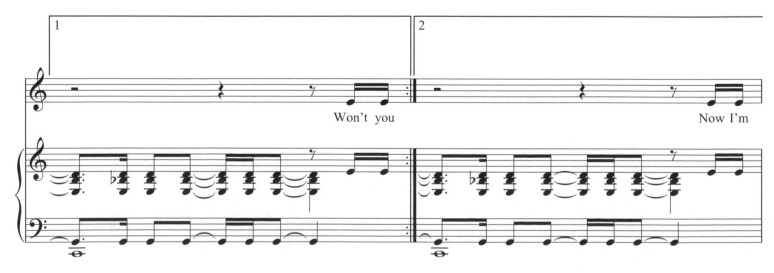

1

Won't you

2

Now I'm

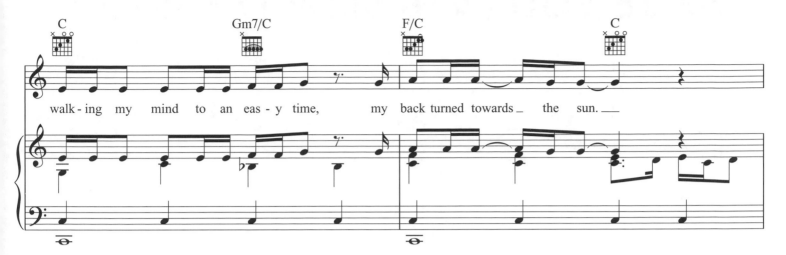

walk-ing my mind to an eas-y time, my back turned towards ___ the sun. ___

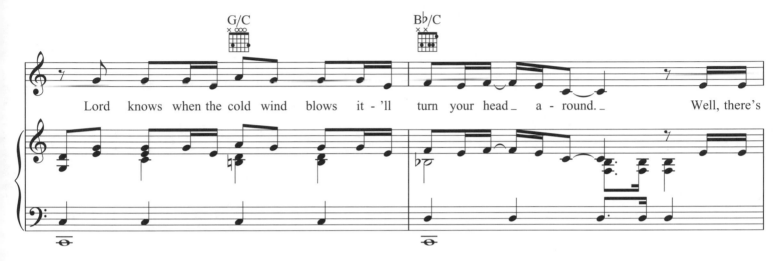

Lord knows when the cold wind blows it - 'll turn your head ___ a - round. ___ Well, there's

hours of time ___ on the tel - e - phone line ___ to talk a - bout things to come, ___

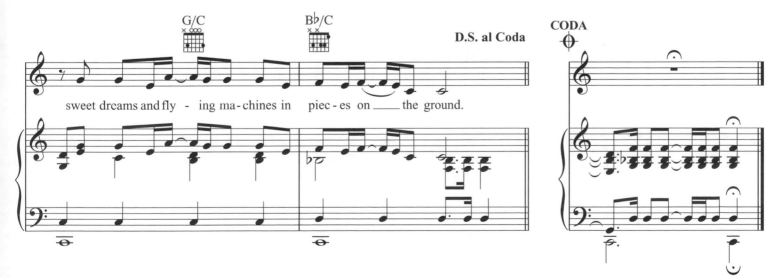

sweet dreams and fly - ing ma-chines in piec - es on ___ the ground.

D.S. al Coda

CODA

HAVE YOU EVER SEEN THE RAIN?

Words and Music by
JOHN FOGERTY

Some-one told me long a - go there's a calm be-fore the storm. I know; and it's been com - in' for some time.

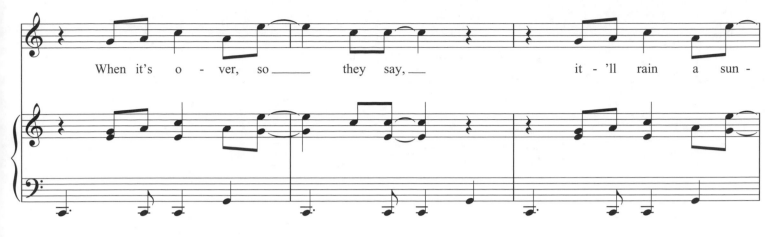

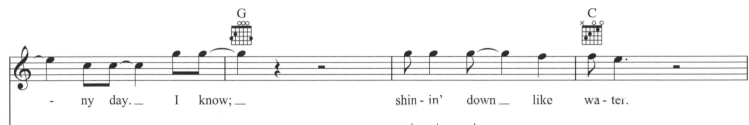

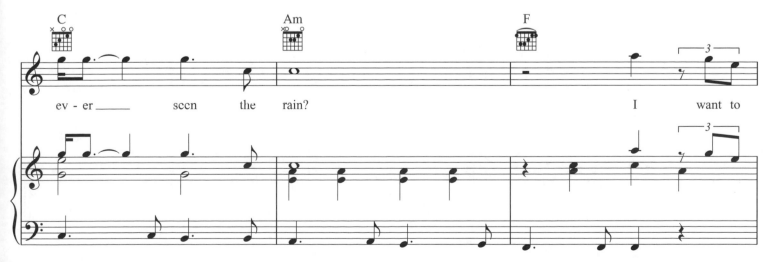

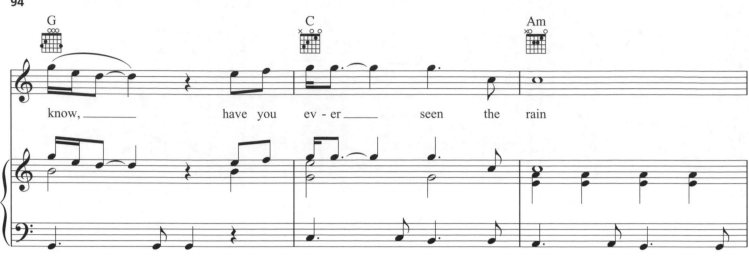

know, _____ have you ev - er _____ seen the rain

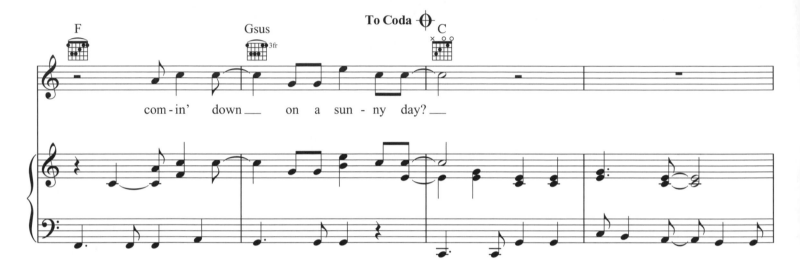

com - in' down _____ on a sun - ny day? _____

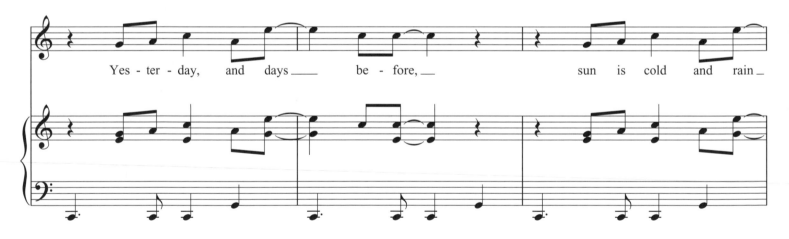

Yes - ter - day, and days _____ be - fore, _____ sun is cold and rain _____

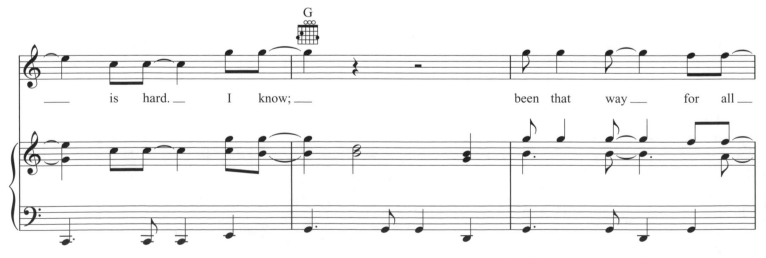

_____ is hard. _____ I know; _____ been that way _____ for all _____

my time. 'Til for - ev - er, on

it goes through the cir - cle, fast and slow. I know;

and it can't stop, I won - der.

D.S. al Coda

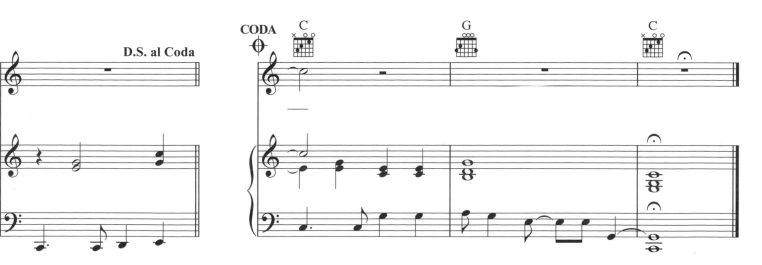

CODA

HOMEWARD BOUND

Words and Music by
PAUL SIMON

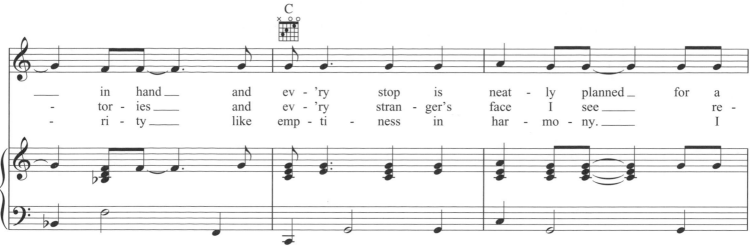

in hand ___ and ev-'ry stop is neat-ly planned ___ for a
-tor - ies ___ and ev-'ry stran - ger's face I see ___ re -
-ri - ty ___ like emp-ti - ness in har - mo - ny. ___ I

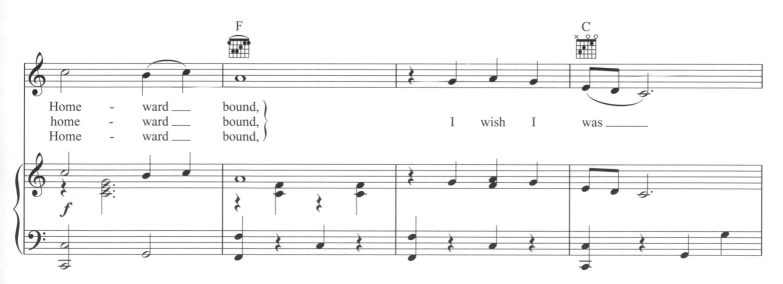

po - et and a one - man band. _____
minds me and that I long to be _____
need some - one to com - fort me. _____

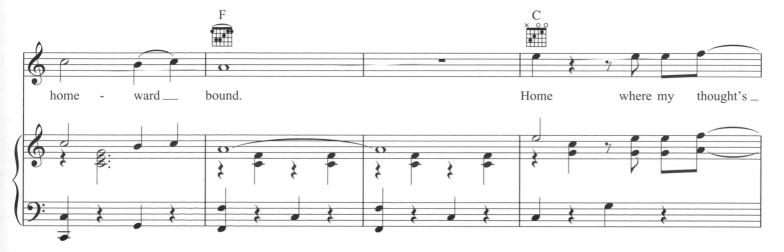

Home - ward ___ bound,
home - ward ___ bound, } I wish I was _____
Home - ward ___ bound,

home - ward ___ bound. Home where my thought's ___

es-cap-ing, home where my mu - sic's play-ing, home where my love

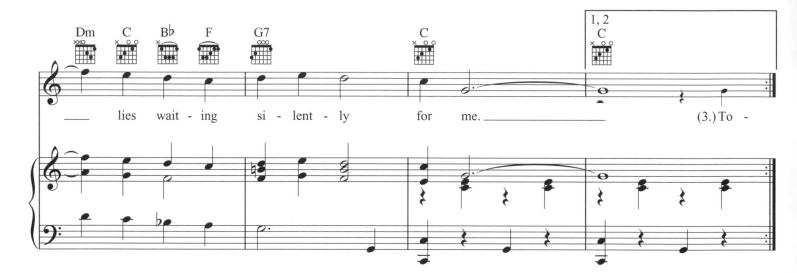

lies wait-ing si - lent-ly for me. (3.) To -

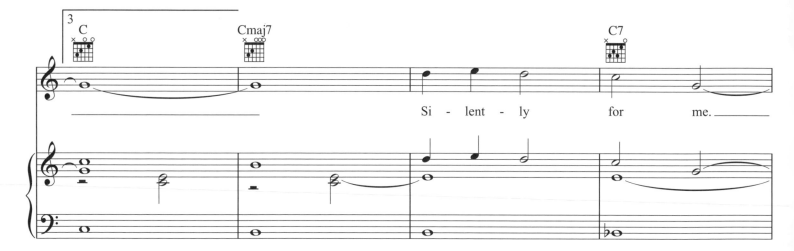

Si - lent - ly for me.

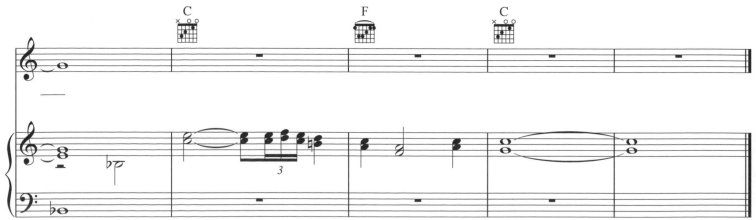

THE JOKER

Words and Music by STEVE MILLER,
EDDIE CURTIS and AHMET ERTEGUN

Moderately

Some peo-ple call me ___ the Space Cow-boy, yeah. ___

Some call me the Gang-ster of Love. ___

Some peo-ple call me ___ Maur - ice 'cause I

speak of the pom-pa-tus of love. _____

Peo-ple talk _ a-bout _____ me, ba - by, _____

say I'm do - ing you wrong, _ do - ing you wrong. _____

Well, don't you wor - ry, ba - by, don't wor - ry 'cause I'm

right here, right here, right here, right here at home.___ 'Cause I'm a

pick-er. I'm a grin-ner. I'm a lov-er and I'm a sin-ner.

I play my mu-sic in___ the sun.___ I'm a

jok-er. I'm a smok-er. I'm a mid-night___ tok-er.

I sure don't want to hurt no one. I'm a

I get my lov-ing on the run. Oo, hoo.

Oo, hoo.

You're the cut - est thing __ that I ev -

- er did see. _____ I real - ly love __ your peach - es, wan - na

shake your tree. _____ Lov-ey dov - ey, lov-ey dov-ey, lov-ey

To Coda ⊕

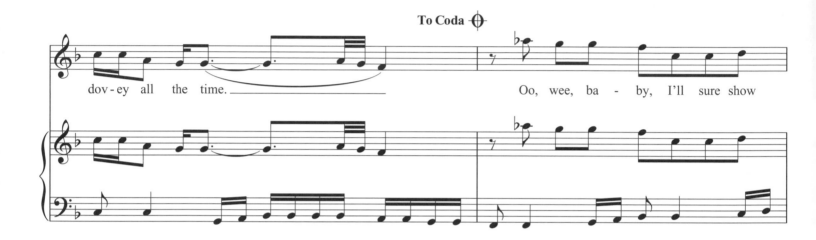

dov-ey all the time. _____ Oo, wee, ba - by, I'll sure show

F   Bb

you a good time. _ 'Cause I'm a pick-er. I'm a grin - ner. I'm a

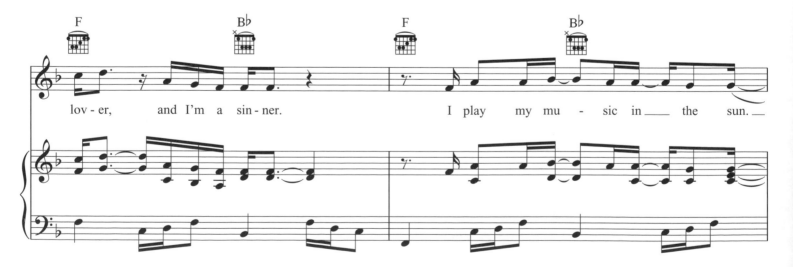

F   Bb   F   Bb

lov-er, and I'm a sin-ner. I play my mu - sic in ___ the sun.

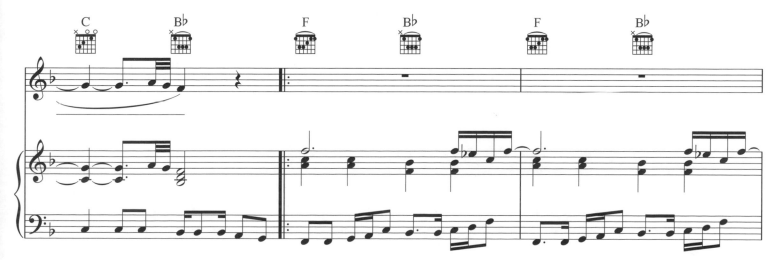

Oo, hoo. Oo, hoo.

People keep talk - in' a - bout ___ me, ba - by.

They say I'm do - ing you wrong. _____

Well, don't you wor-ry. Don't wor-ry. No, don't wor-ry, ma - ma,

D.S. al Coda

'cause I'm right here at home.

CODA

Come on, babe, __ and I'll show you a good time.

Repeat and Fade | **Optional Ending**

A HORSE WITH NO NAME

Words and Music by
DEWEY BUNNELL

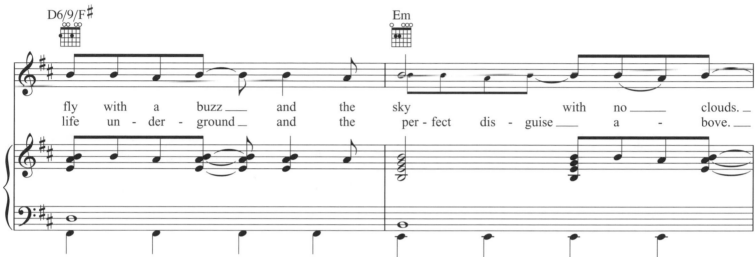

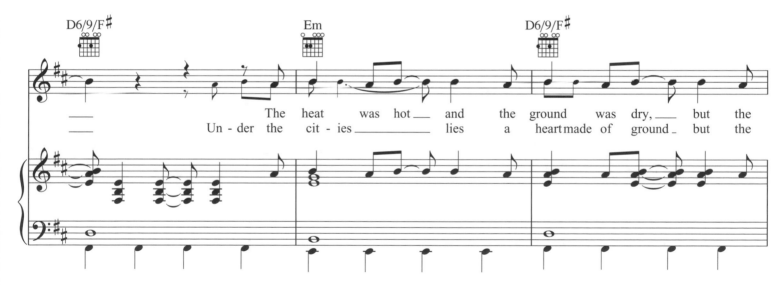

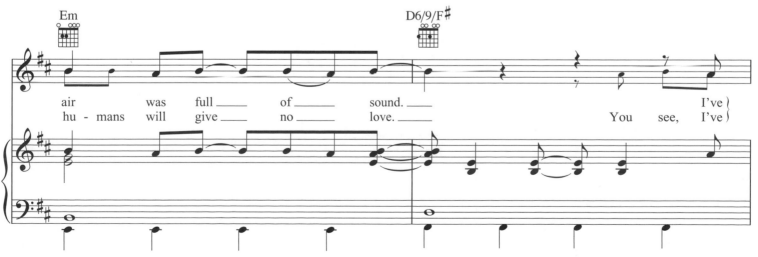

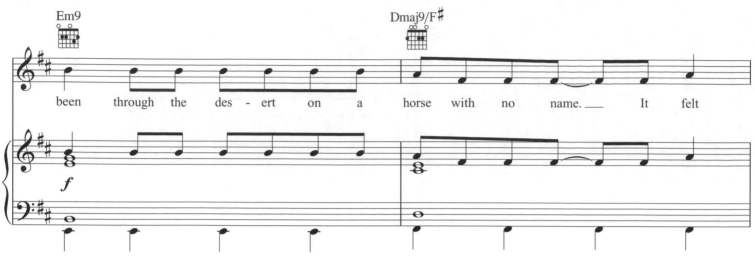

been through the des-ert on a horse with no name.___ It felt

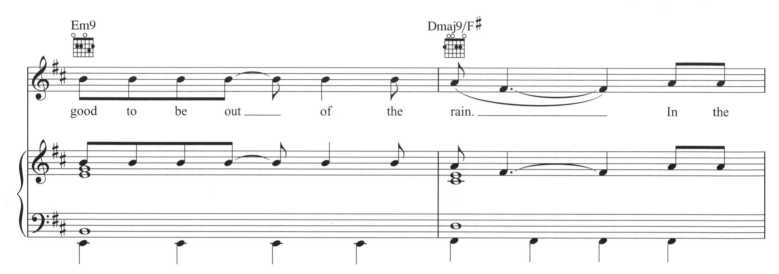

good to be out ___ of the rain. ___ In the

des-ert ___ you can re-mem-ber your name ___ 'cause there

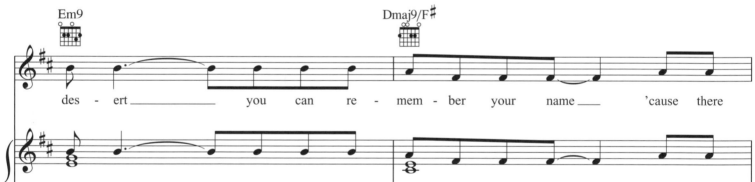

To Coda ⊕

ain't no one for to give you no pain. ___ La la la

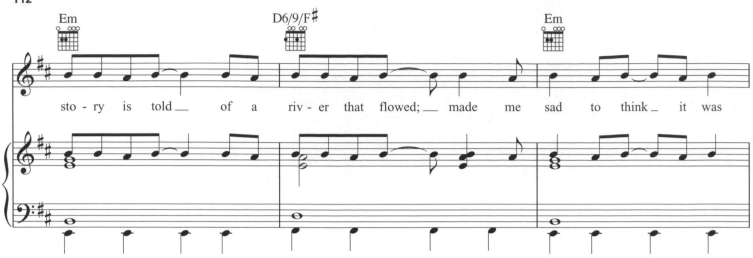

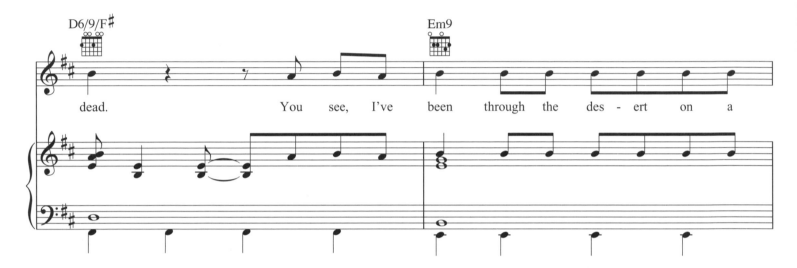

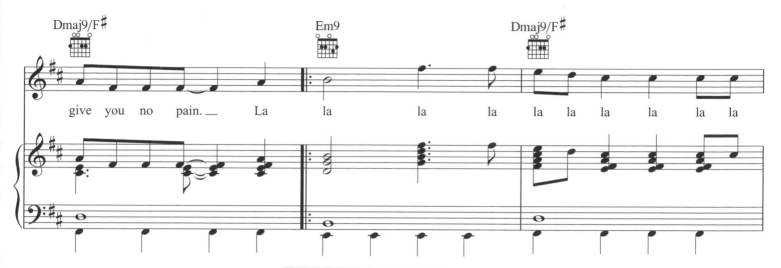

give you no pain. ___ La la la la la la la la la la

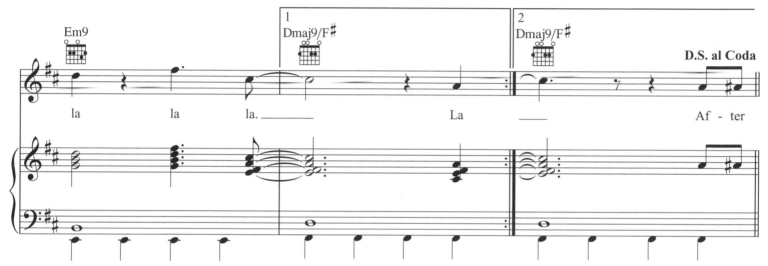

la la la. ___ La ___ Af - ter

D.S. al Coda

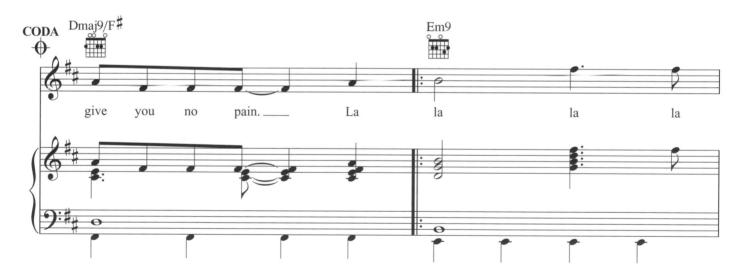

give you no pain. ___ La la la la

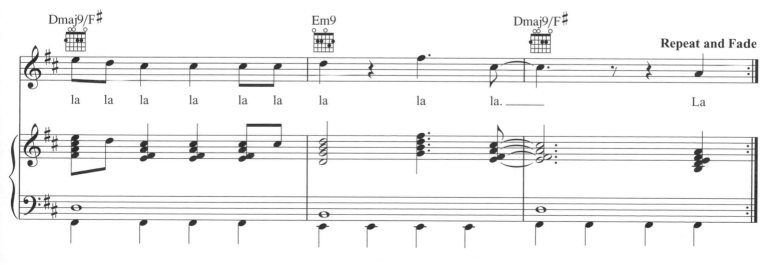

la la la la la la la la. ___ La

Repeat and Fade

IF

Words and Music by
DAVID GATES

Moderately, with feeling

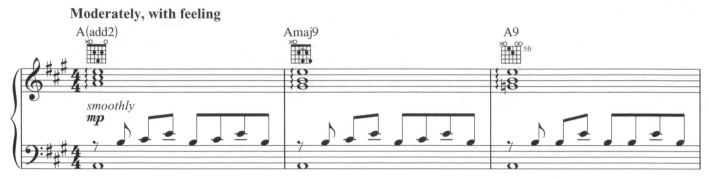

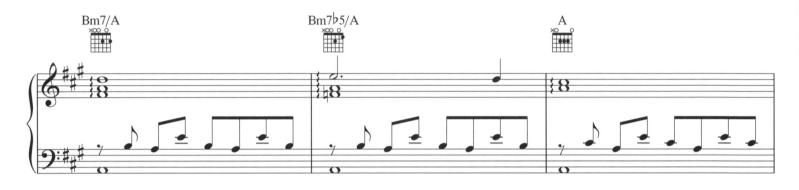

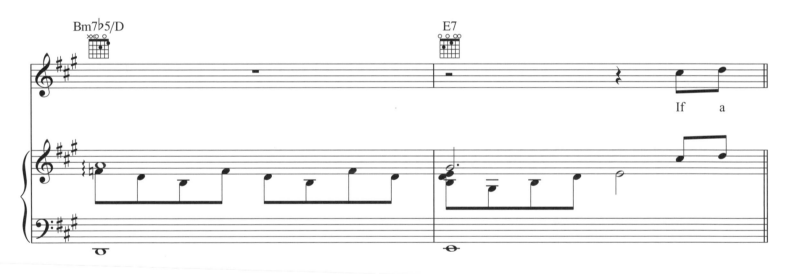

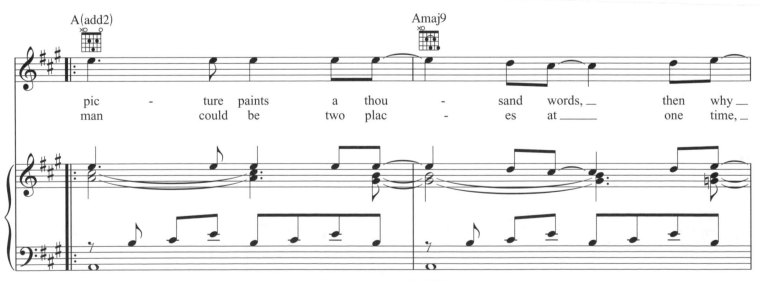

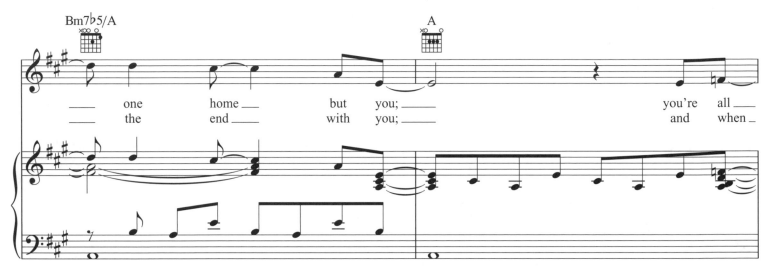

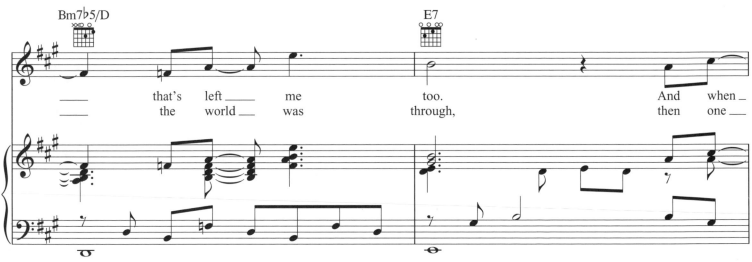

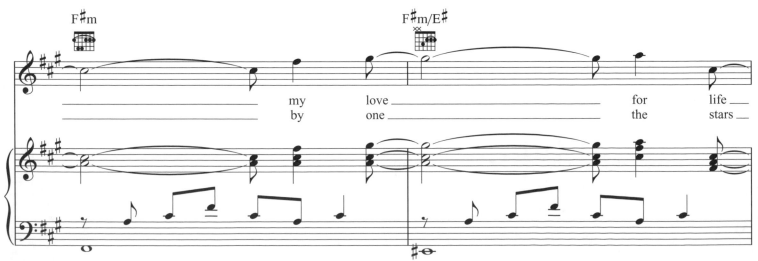

JOLENE

Words and Music by
DOLLY PARTON

voice is soft like sum - mer rain, and I can - not com - pete with you, ___
hap - pi - ness de - pends on you and what - ev - er you de - cide to do, ___

To Coda ⊕

Jo - lene. He
Jo - lene. Jo -

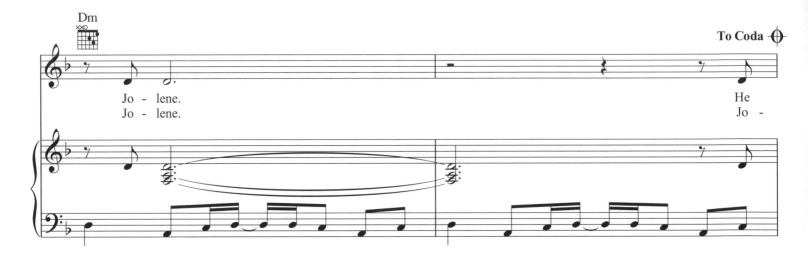

talks a - bout you in his sleep and there's noth - ing I can do to keep from

cry - in' when he calls your name, Jo - lene. ___ And

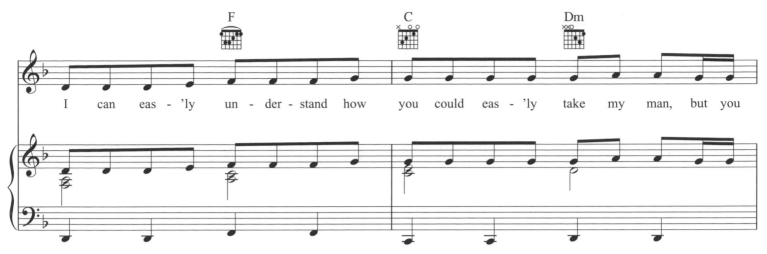

I can eas-'ly un-der-stand how you could eas-'ly take my man, but you

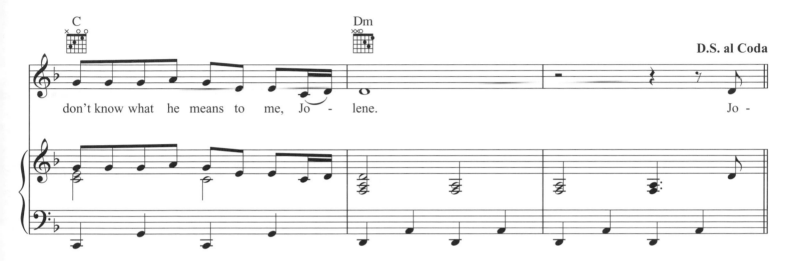

D.S. al Coda

don't know what he means to me, Jo - lene. Jo -

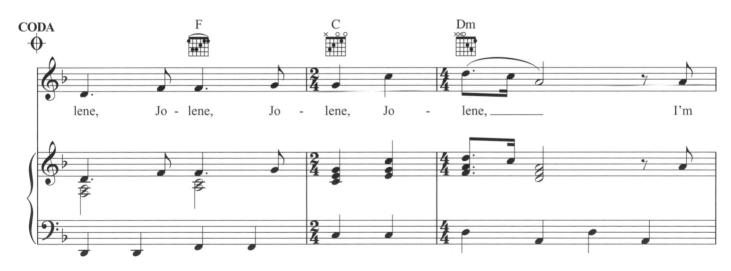

CODA

lene, Jo - lene, Jo - lene, Jo - lene, _____ I'm

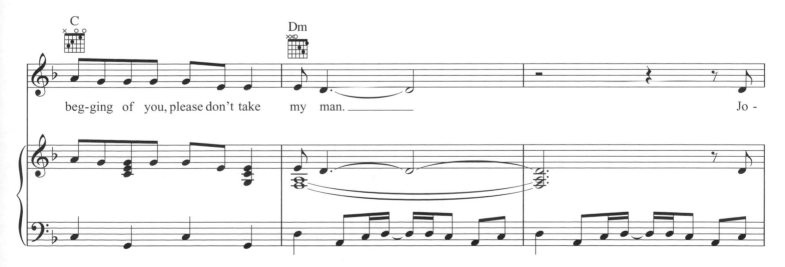

beg-ging of you, please don't take my man. _____ Jo -

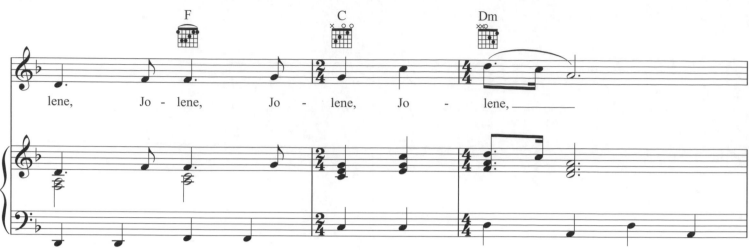

lene, Jo - lene, Jo - lene, Jo - lene, _____

please don't take him just be-cause you can. _____ Jo-

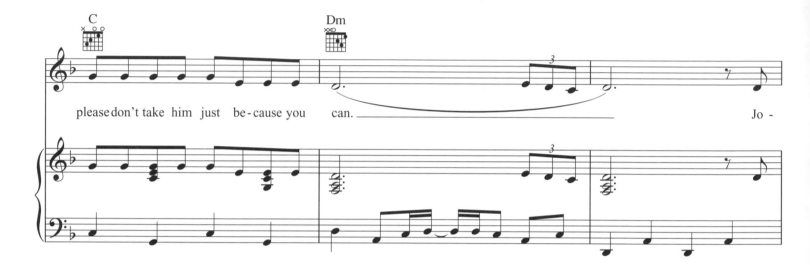

lene, Jo - lene, please don't take my man, Jo - lene, Jo-

lene, Jo - lene. My hap - pi - ness de-pends on you, Jo - lene.

LEARNING TO FLY

Words and Music by TOM PETTY
and JEFF LYNNE

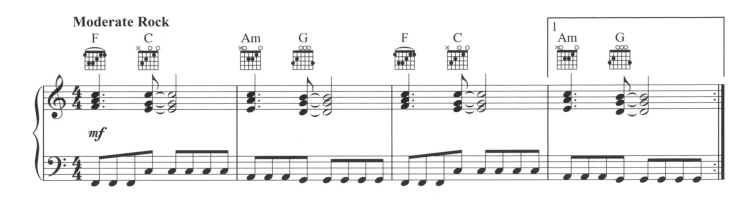

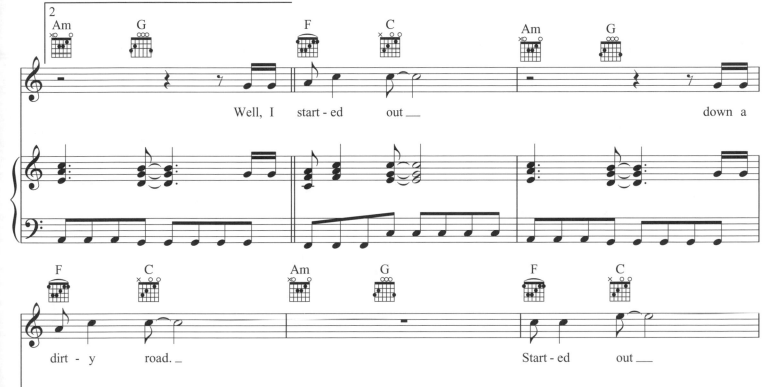

Well, I start-ed out _____ down a

dirt-y road. _____ Start-ed out _____

all a - lone. _____ And the

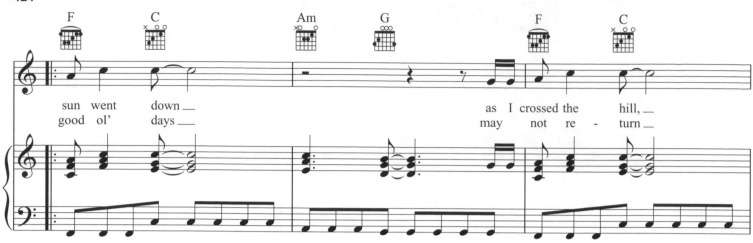

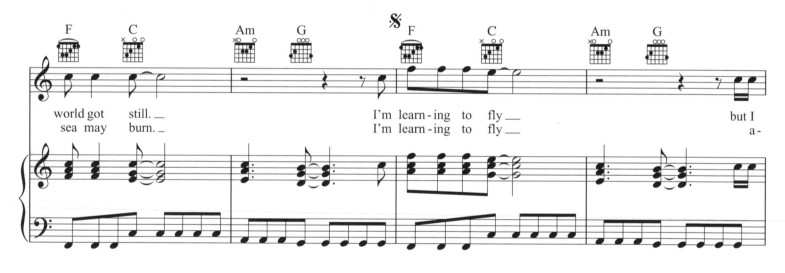

hard - est thing. __
must   come   down. __

Well, the

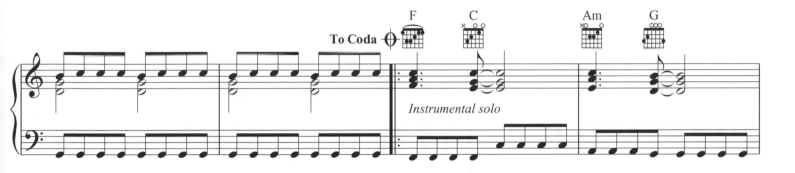

Instrumental solo

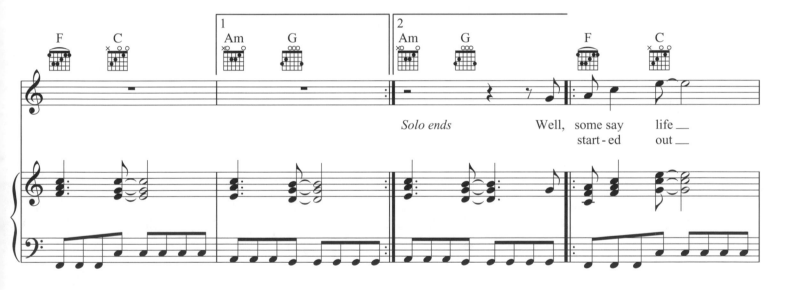

Solo ends

Well,   some say   life __
          start - ed   out __

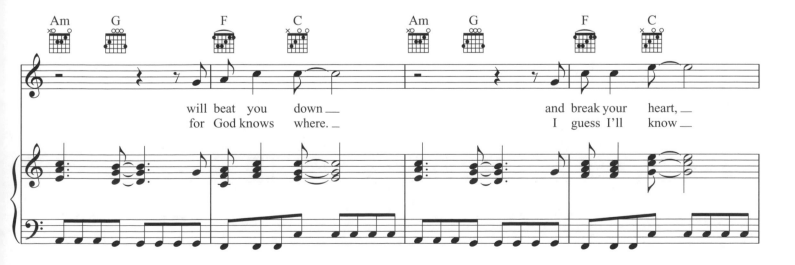

will beat   you   down __
for   God knows   where. __

and break your   heart, __
I   guess I'll   know __

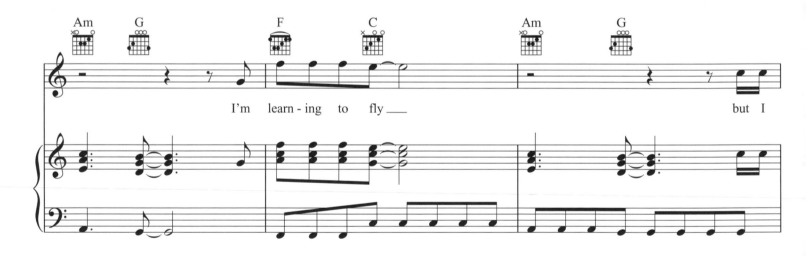

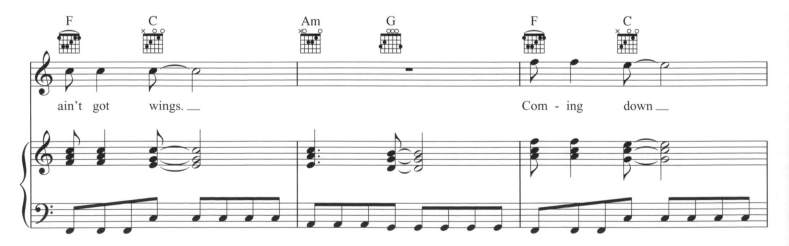

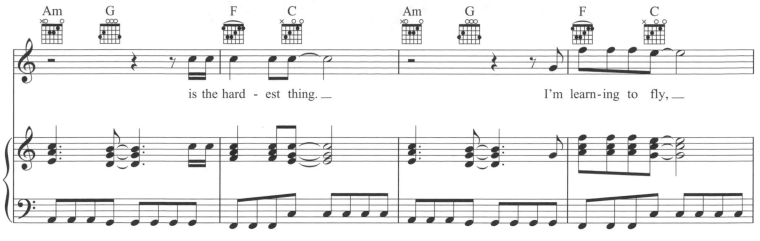

is the hard - est thing. ___ I'm learn-ing to fly, ___

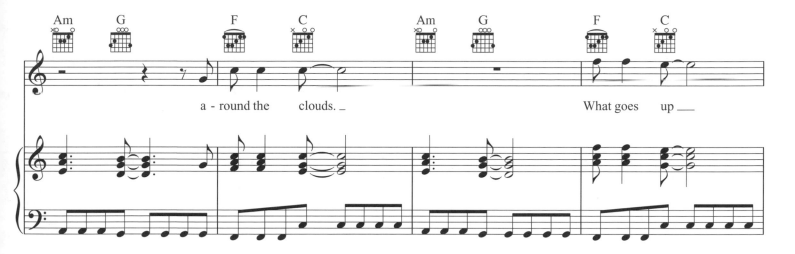

a - round the clouds. ___ What goes up ___

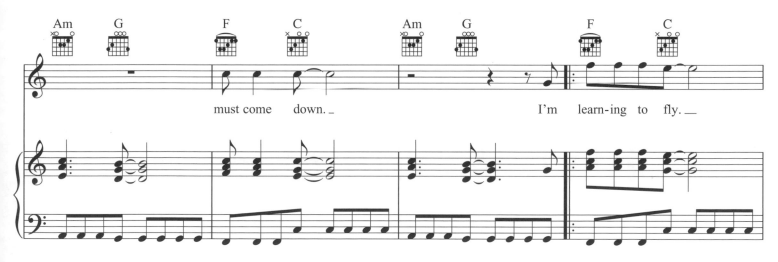

must come down. ___ I'm learn-ing to fly. ___

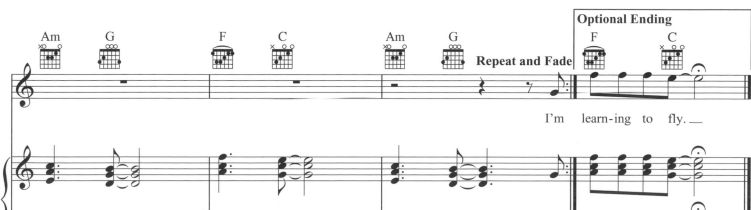

Optional Ending

Repeat and Fade

I'm learn-ing to fly. ___

LEAVING ON A JET PLANE

Words and Music by
JOHN DENVER

Moderately

All my bags are packed, __ I'm read-y to go. I'm
man-y times __ I've let you down; so
Now the time __ has come to leave you;

stand-ing here __ out-side your door. __ I hate to wake __ you
man-y times __ I've played a-round. __ I tell you now:
one more time __ let me kiss you. Then close your eyes,

up to say __ good-bye. But the
they don't mean __ a thing. Ev-'ry
I'll be on __ my way.

dawn is break - in', it's ear - ly morn. The tax - i's wait - in', he's
place I go ___ I'll think of you. ___ Ev - 'ry song I sing ___ I'll
Dream a - bout ___ the days to come, ___ when I won't have ___ to

blow - in' his horn. ___ Al - read - y I'm so lone - some I could
sing ___ for you. ___ When I come back, I'll bring your wed - ding
leave ___ a - lone. ___ A - bout the times I won't have to

die. _____
ring. _____
say: _____ So kiss me and smile for me. ___

Tell me that ___ you'll wait for me. ___ Hold me like ___ you'll nev - er let me go. ___

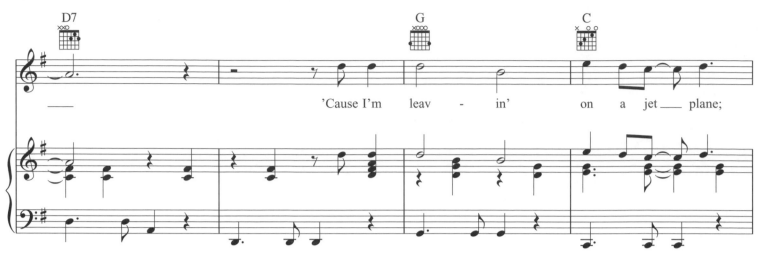

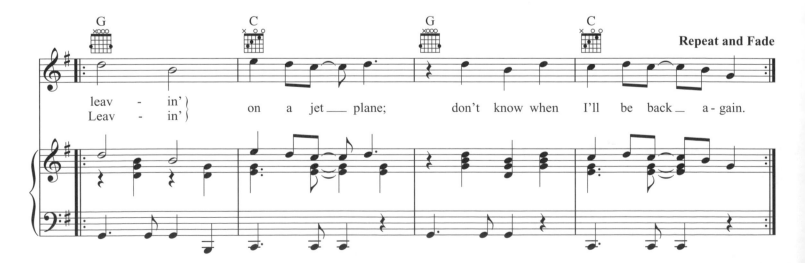

MORE THAN A FEELING

Words and Music by
TOM SCHOLZ

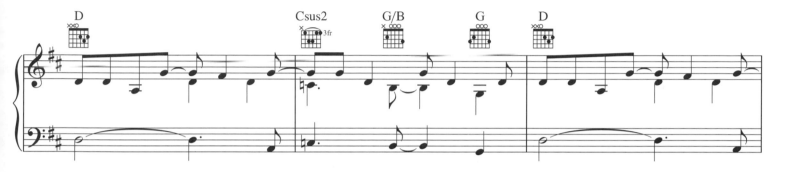

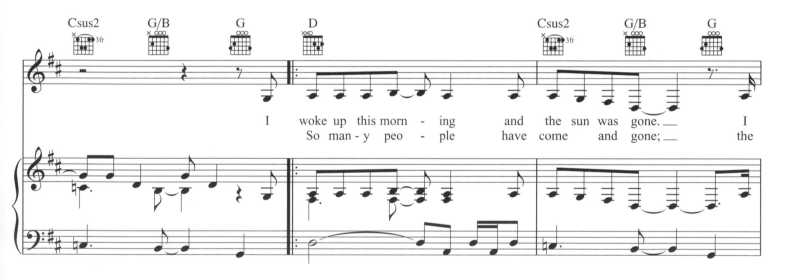

I woke up this morn - ing and the sun was gone. __ I
So man - y peo - ple have come and gone; __ the

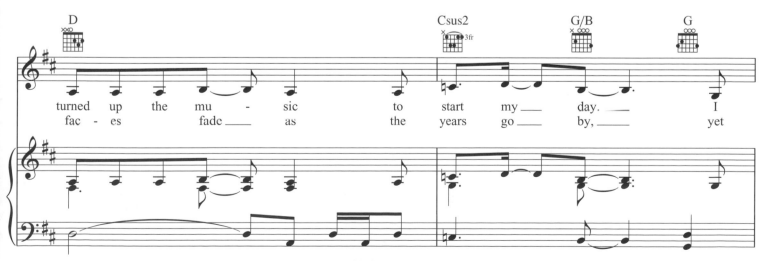

turned up the mu - sic to start my __ day. __ I
fac - es fade __ as the years go __ by, __ yet

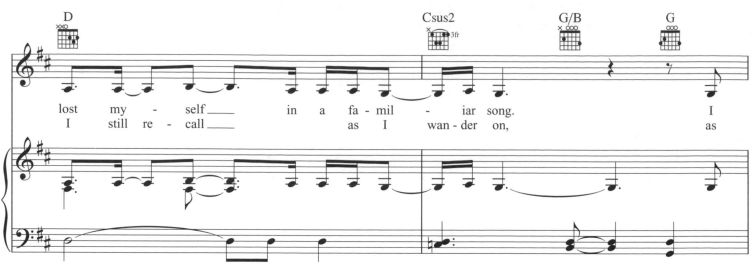

lost my - self ____ in a fa - mil - iar song.
I still re - call ____ as I wan - der on,

I
as

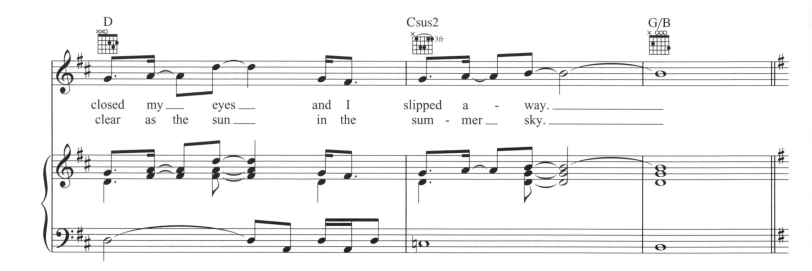

closed my ____ eyes ____ and I slipped a - way. _____
clear as the sun ____ in the sum - mer ____ sky. _____

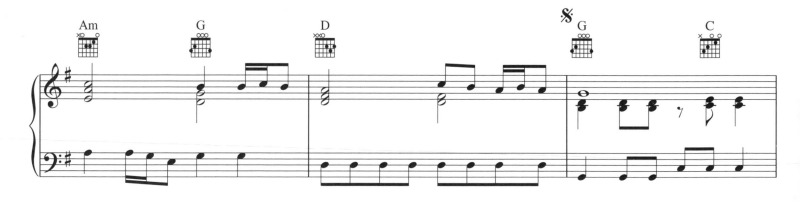

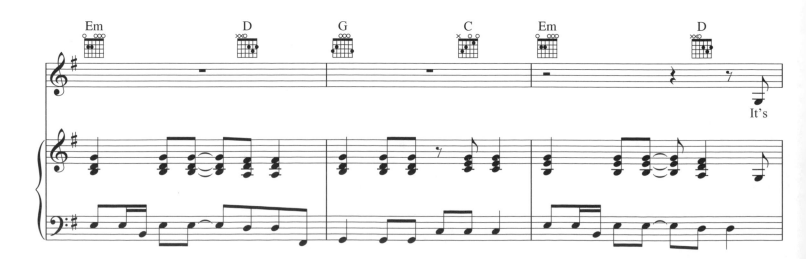

It's

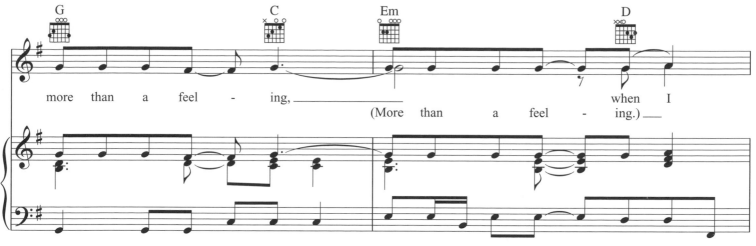

more than a feel - ing, _____ (More than a feel - ing.) _____ when I

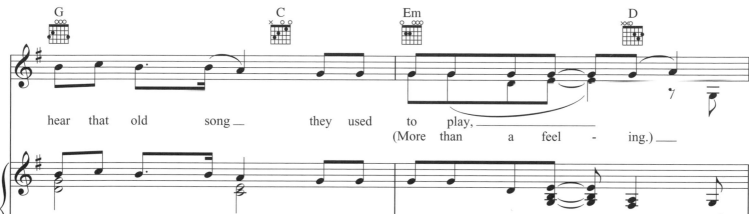

hear that old song _____ they used to play, _____ (More than a feel - ing.) _____ and

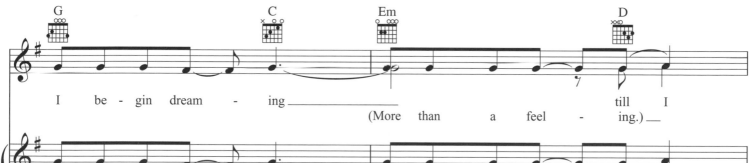

I be - gin dream - ing _____ (More than a feel - ing.) _____ till I

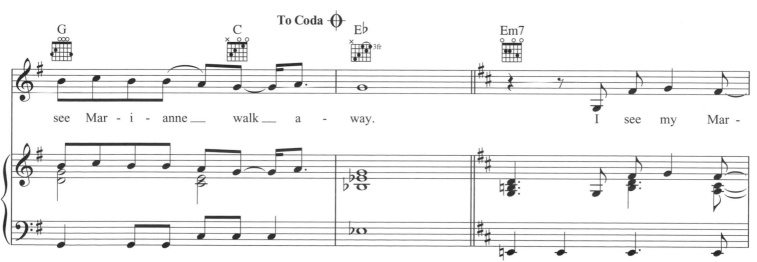

see Mar - i - anne _____ walk _____ a - way. I see my Mar -

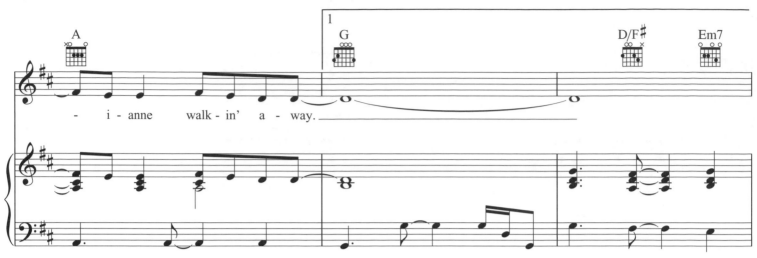

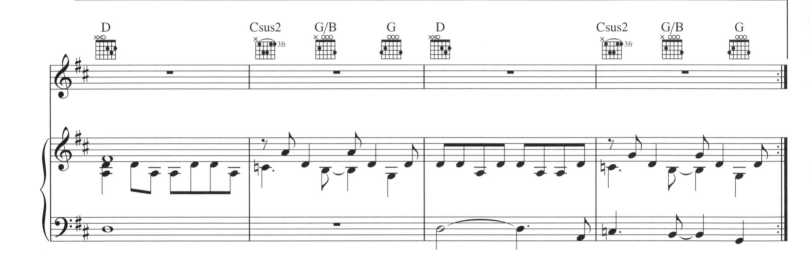

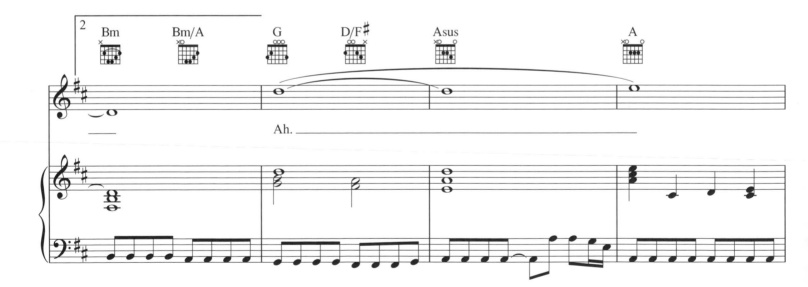

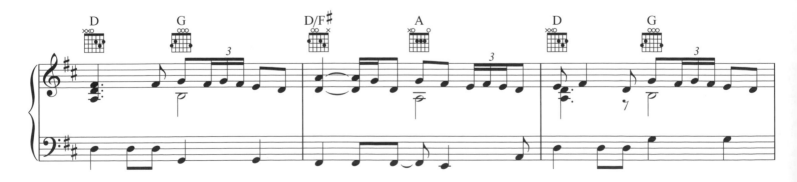

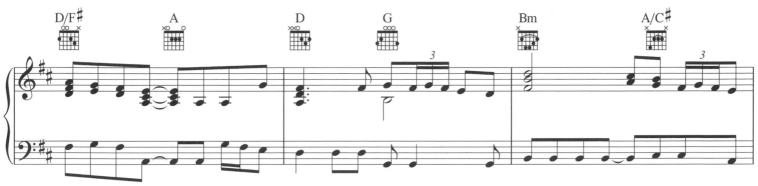

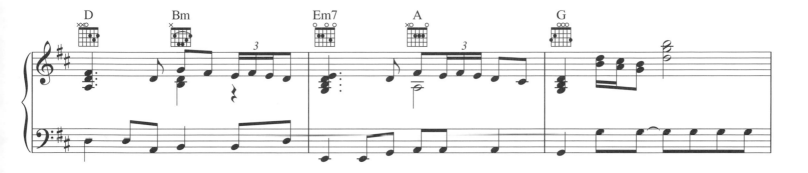

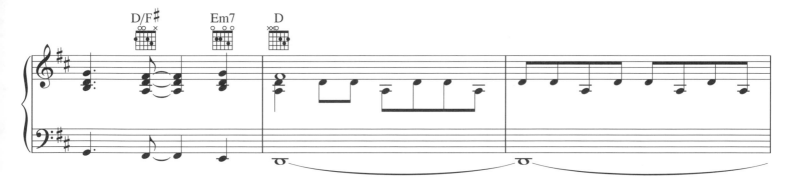

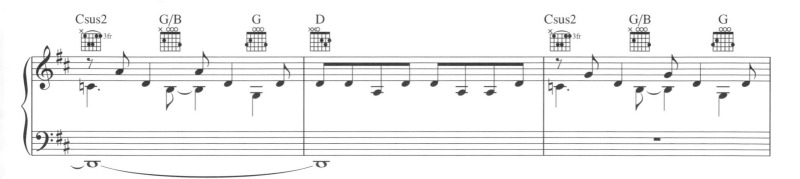

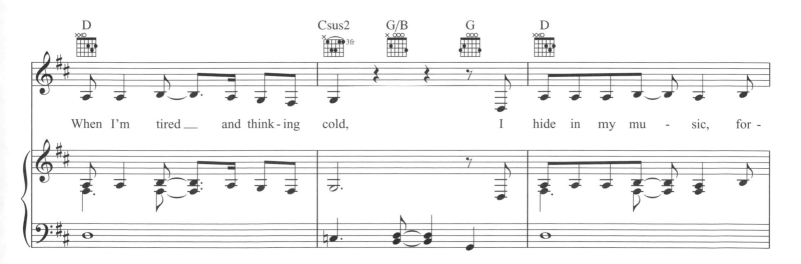

When I'm tired ___ and think-ing cold, I hide in my mu - sic, for -

get the __ day __ and dream of a girl __ I used to know. __ I

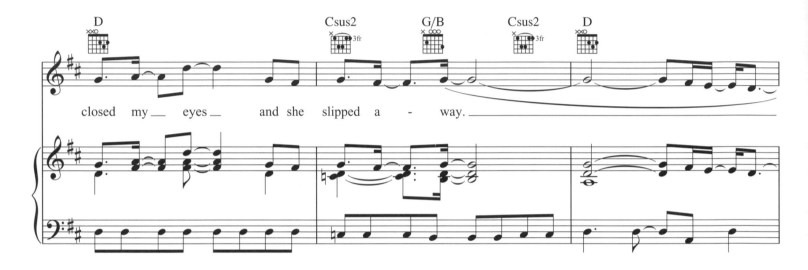

closed my __ eyes __ and she slipped a - way. _____

_____ She slipped a - way. _____

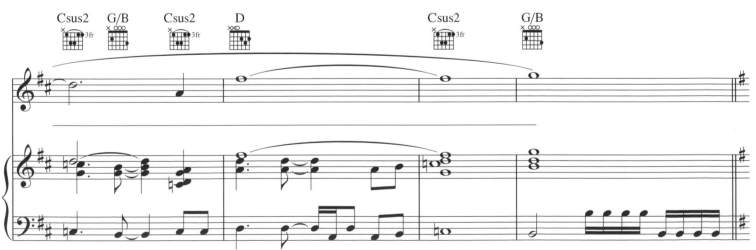

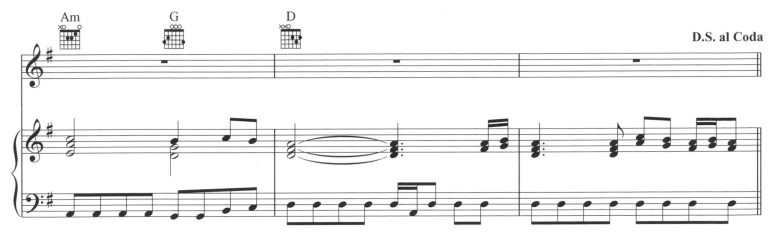

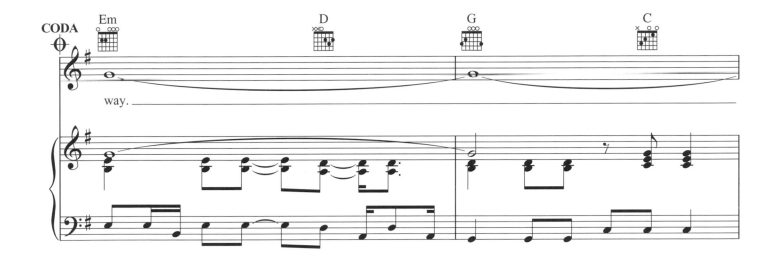

way. _____

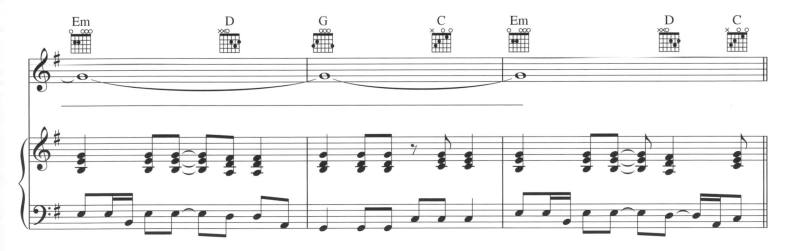

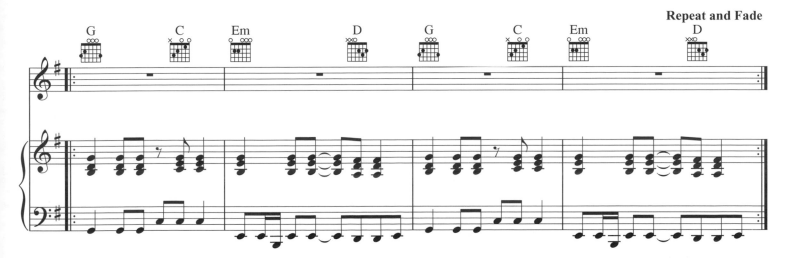

LONGER

Words and Music by
DAN FOGELBERG

Moderate Ballad

Long - er than _ there've been fish - es in the o - cean,
Strong - er than _ an - y moun - tain ca - the - dral,
Through the years _ as the fi - re starts to mel - low,

high - er than _ an - y bird ev - er flew, _ long - er than _ there've been
tru - er than _ an - y tree ev - er grew, _ deep - er than _ an - y
burn - ing lines _ in the book of our lives, _ though the bind - ing cracks _ and the

I'll be in love __ with you. __

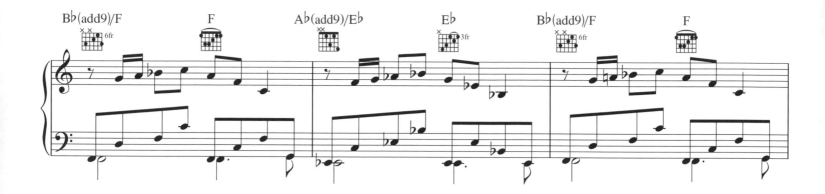

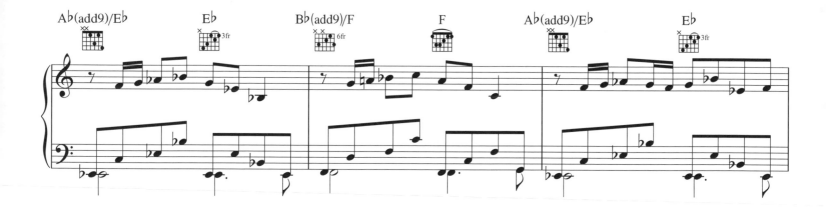

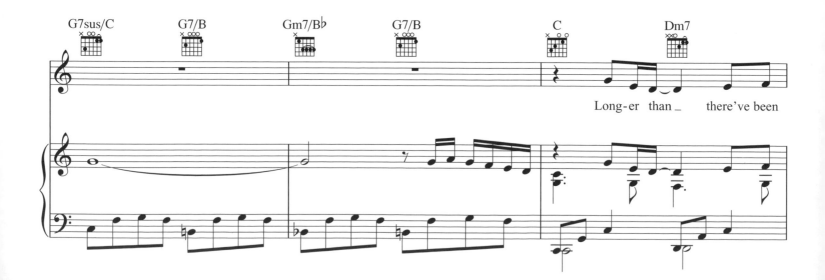

Long-er than __ there've been

fish - es ___ in the o - cean, ___ high-er than ___ an - y bird ev - er flew, ___

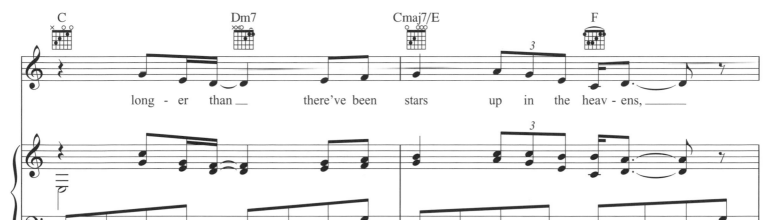

long - er than ___ there've been stars up in the heav - ens, ___

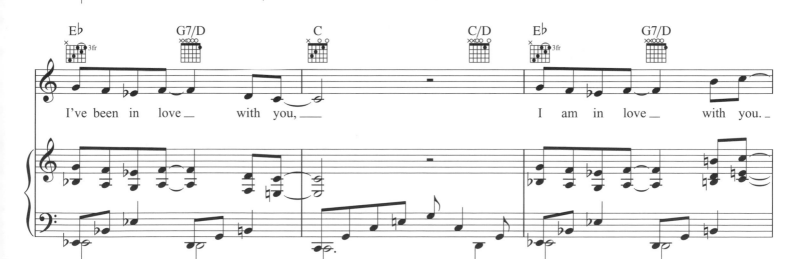

I've been in love ___ with you, ___ I am in love ___ with you. ___

MAGGIE MAY

Words and Music by ROD STEWART
and MARTIN QUITTENTON

that don't wor-ry me none; in my eyes you're ev - 'ry - thing. I

laughed at all of your jokes, my love you did-n't need to coax. _____ Oh,

Mag - gie, I could - n't have tried _____ an - y - more.

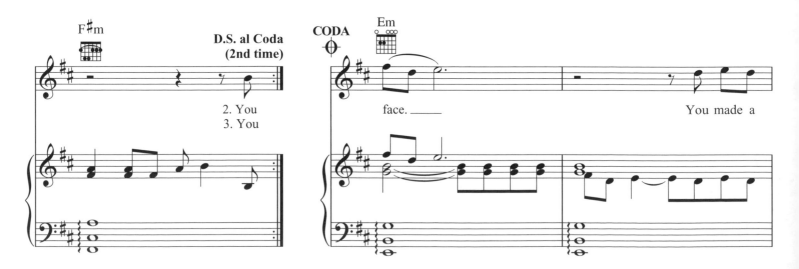

D.S. al Coda (2nd time)

2. You
3. You

CODA

face. _____

You made a

Additional Lyrics

2. You lured me away from home, just to save you from being alone.
   You stole my soul, that's a pain I can do without.
   All I needed was a friend to lend a guiding hand.
   But you turned into a lover, and, mother, what a lover! You wore me out.
   All you did was wreck my bed and in the morning kick me in the head.
   Oh, Maggie, I couldn't have tried anymore.

3. You lured me away from home 'cause you didn't want to be alone.
   You stole my heart, I couldn't leave you if I tried.
   I suppose I could collect my books and get back to school,
   Or steal my daddy's cue and make a living out of playing pool,
   Or find myself a rock and roll band that needs a helpin' hand.
   Oh, Maggie, I wish I'd never seen your face. *(To Coda)*

ME AND BOBBY McGEE

Words and Music by KRIS KRISTOFFERSON
and FRED FOSTER

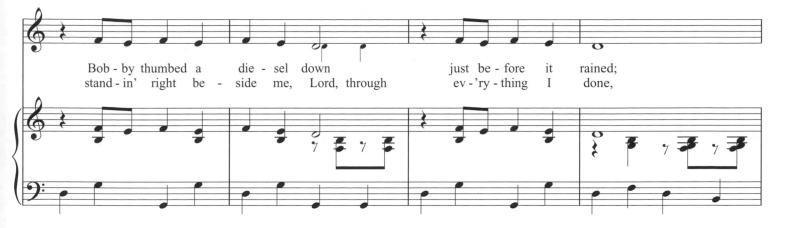

Bob - by thumbed a die - sel down just be - fore it rained;
stand - in' right be - side me, Lord, through ev - 'ry - thing I done,

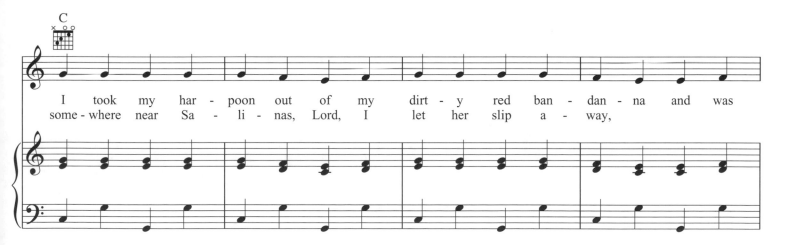

C6

took us all the way to New Or - leans.
ev - 'ry night she kept me from the cold.

Then

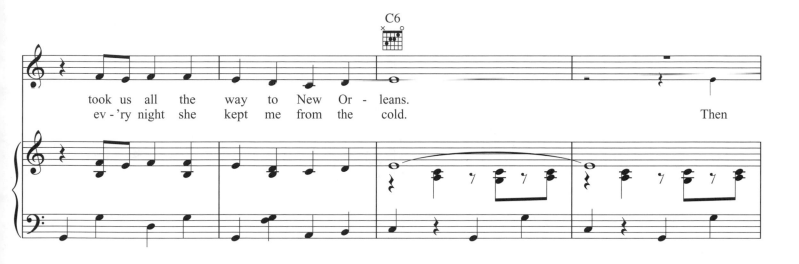

C

I took my har - poon out of my dirt - y red ban - dan - na and was
some - where near Sa - li - nas, Lord, I let her slip a - way,

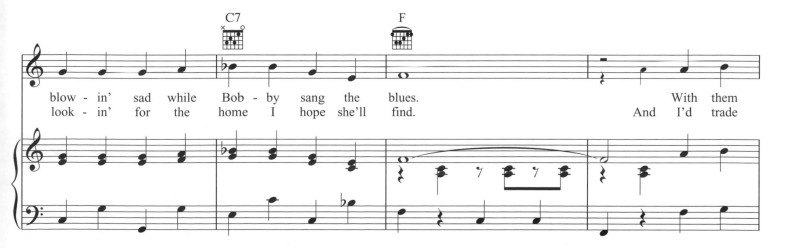

C7   F

blow - in' sad while Bob - by sang the blues.
look - in' for the home I hope she'll find.

With them
And I'd trade

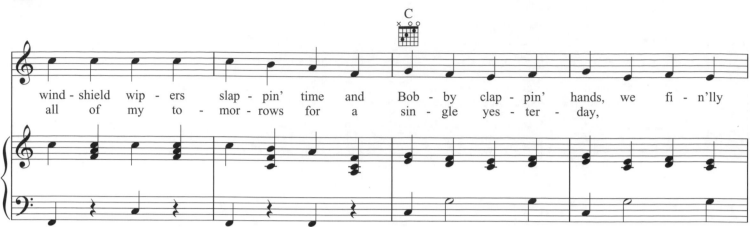

wind - shield wip - ers slap - pin' time and Bob - by clap - pin' hands, we fi - n'lly
all of my to - mor - rows for a sin - gle yes - ter - day,

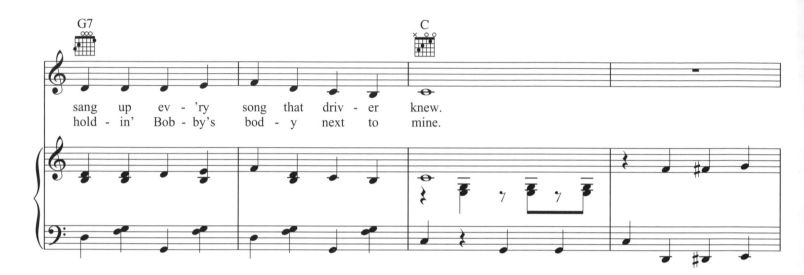

sang up ev - 'ry song that driv - er knew.
hold - in' Bob - by's bod - y next to mine.

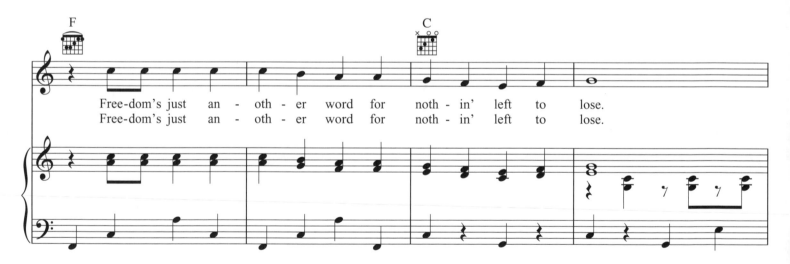

Free - dom's just an - oth - er word for noth - in' left to lose.
Free - dom's just an - oth - er word for noth - in' left to lose.

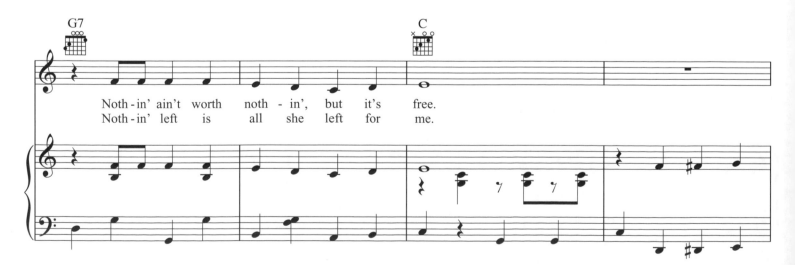

Noth - in' ain't worth noth - in', but it's free.
Noth - in' left is all she left for me.

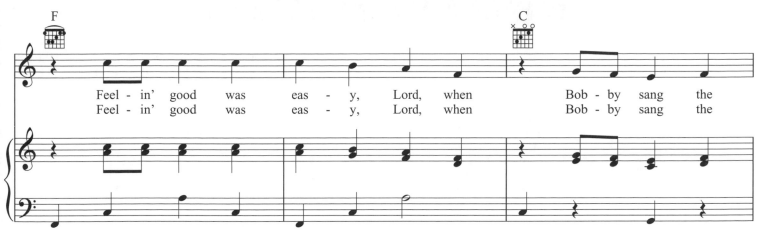

Feel - in' good was eas - y, Lord, when Bob - by sang the
Feel - in' good was eas - y, Lord, when Bob - by sang the

blues; and feel - in' good was good e - nough for me,
blues; And, bud - dy, that was good e - nough for me,

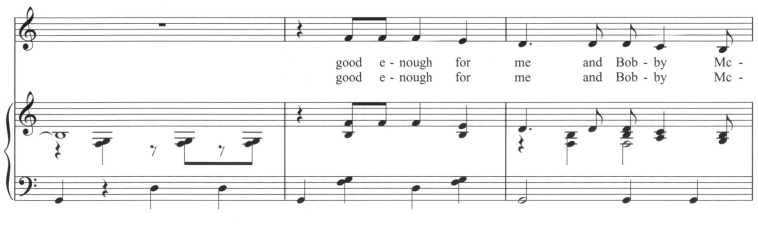

good e - nough for me and Bob - by Mc -
good e - nough for me and Bob - by Mc -

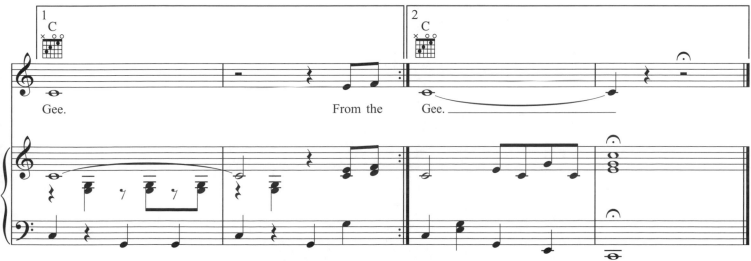

Gee. From the Gee.

NEW KID IN TOWN

Words and Music by JOHN DAVID SOUTHER,
DON HENLEY and GLENN FREY

There's talk on the street; ___
You look in her eyes; ___

___ it sounds so fa - mil - iar.
___ the mu - sic be - gins to play.

John - ny - come - late - ly, the new kid in
John - ny - come - late - ly, the new kid in

town. Ev - 'ry - bod - y loves _ you, so don't _ let them
town. Will she still love _ you

down. _ when you're not a - round? _

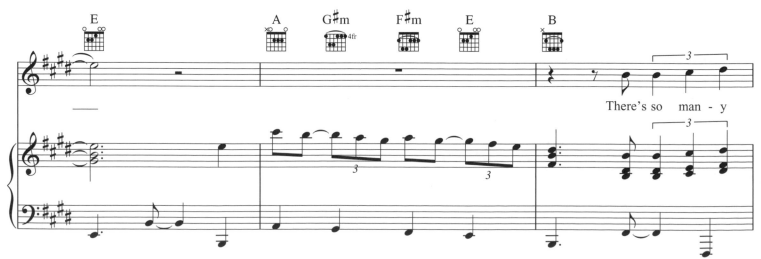

There's so man - y

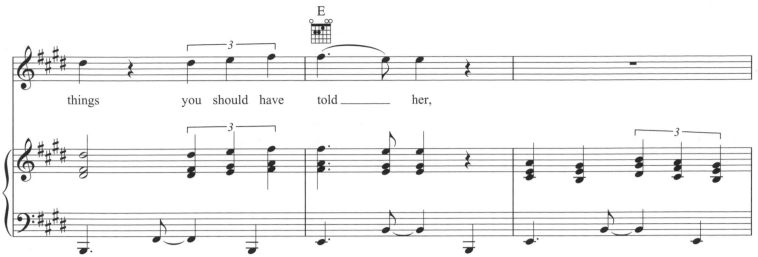

things you should have told _____ her,

but night af - ter night you're will - ing to hold _____ her, just

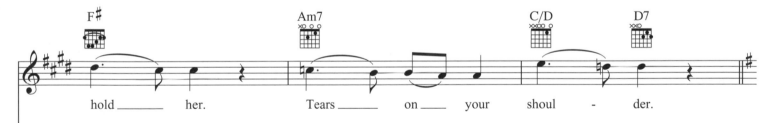

hold _____ her. Tears _____ on _____ your shoul - der.

There's talk on the street; it's there to re - mind _____ you

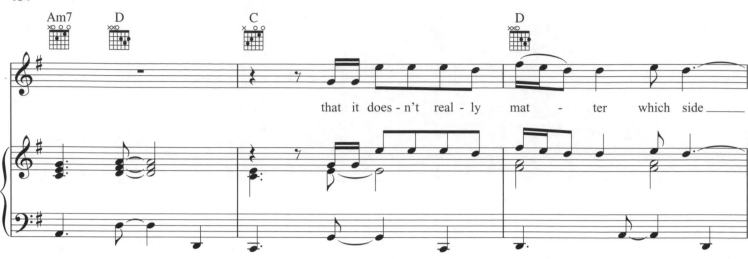

that it does-n't real-ly mat - ter which side _____

_____ you're on. _____ You're walk-ing a - way _____

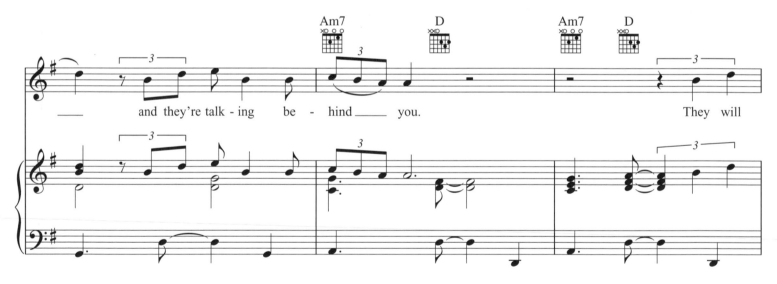

_____ and they're talk-ing be - hind _____ you. They will

nev - er for - get you till some-bod - y new comes a - long. _____

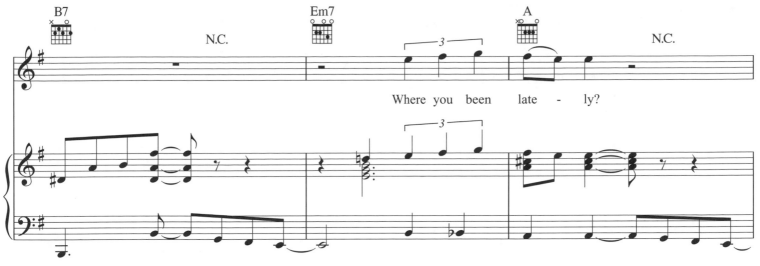

Where you been late - ly?

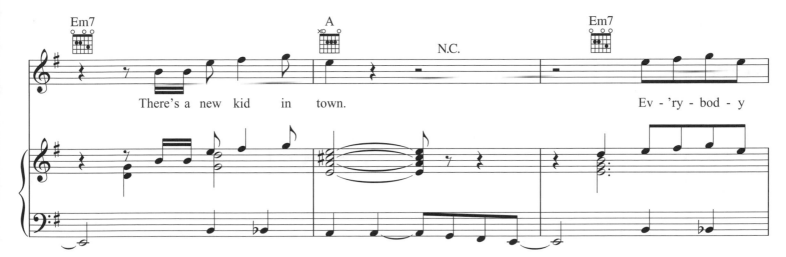

There's a new kid in town.

Ev - 'ry - bod - y

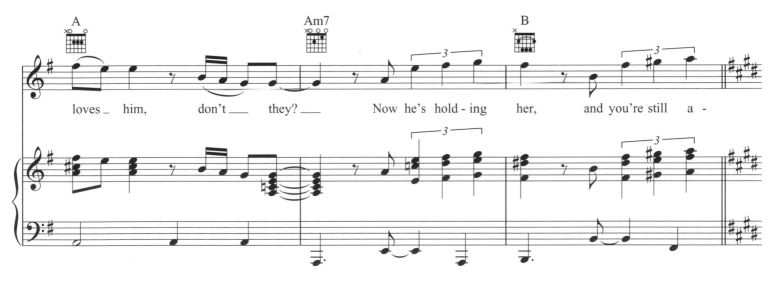

loves_ him, don't_ they?_ Now he's hold - ing her, and you're still a -

round._ Oh, my,_ my._

Ooh, _____ hoo. Ev - 'ry - bod - y's walk - ing like the new kid in town.

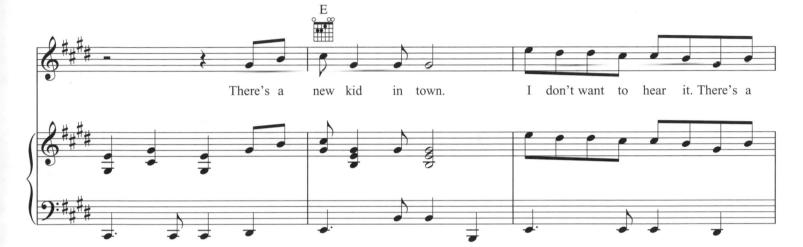

There's a new kid in town. I don't want to hear it. There's a

new kid in town. I_____ don't want to hear it. There's a new kid in town.

There's a new kid in town. There's a

Repeat and Fade

NIGHT MOVES

Words and Music by
BOB SEGER

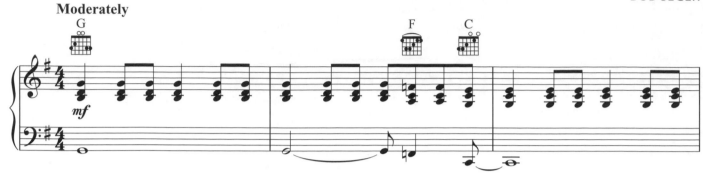

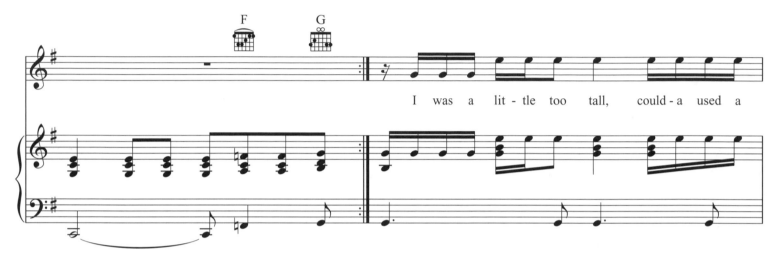

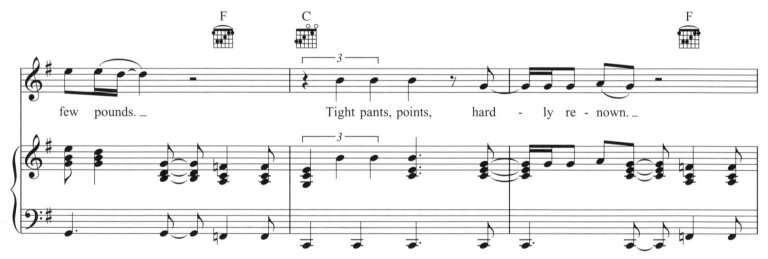

and points all her own, _ sit-tin' way up high, _

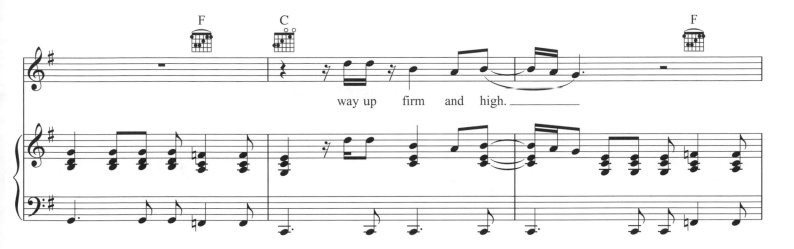

way up firm and high. _

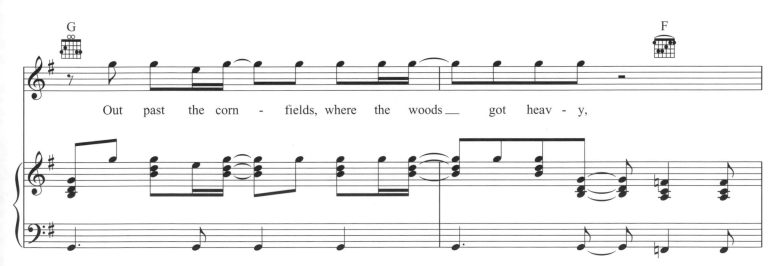

Out past the corn - fields, where the woods __ got heav-y,

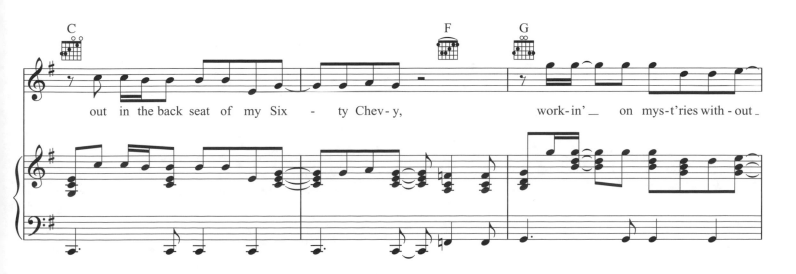

out in the back seat of my Six - ty Chev-y, work-in' _ on mys-t'ries with-out _

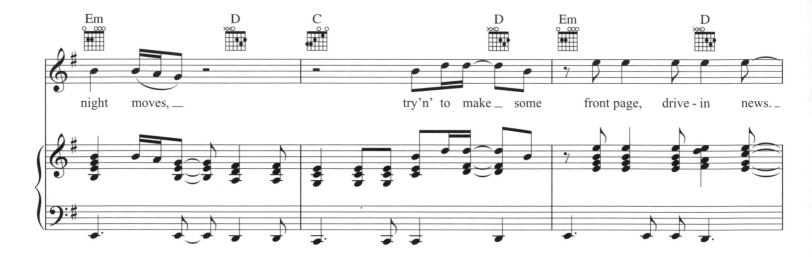

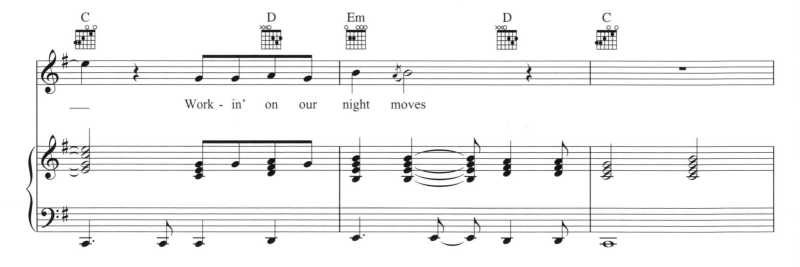

in the sweet ___ sum-mer-time. ___

We were-n't in love. Oh,

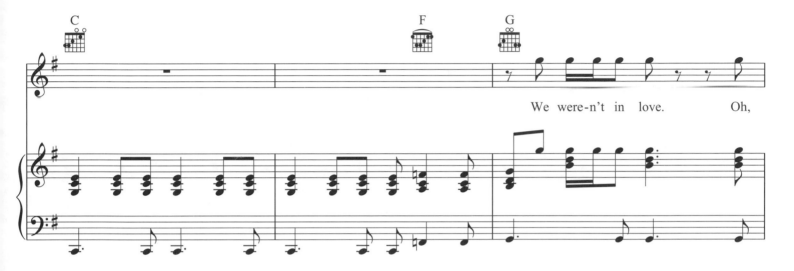

no, far from it. We were-n't search - in for some pie - in-the - sky sum - mit.

We were just ___ young and ___ rest - less and bored, ___ liv-ing by the sword. ___

And we'd steal a - way ev - 'ry chance we could,

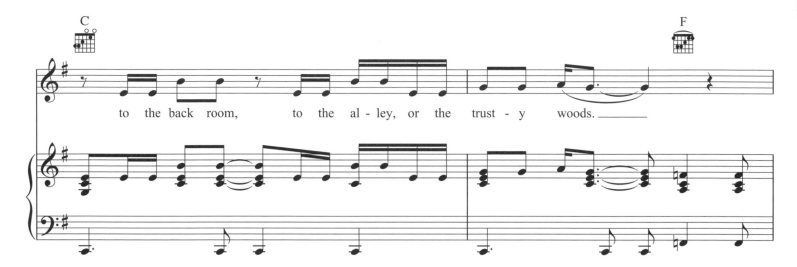

to the back room, to the al - ley, or the trust - y woods. _____

I used her, she used me, ___ but nei - ther one cared. _____

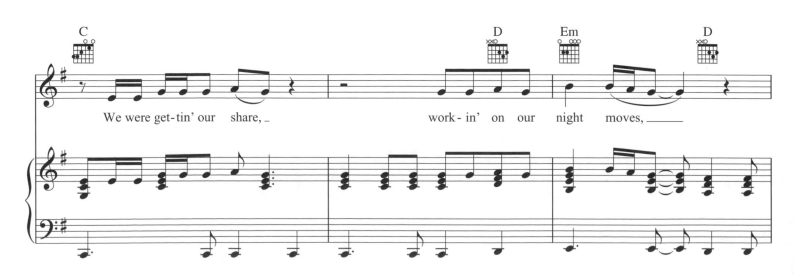

We were get - tin' our share, __ work - in' on our night moves, _____

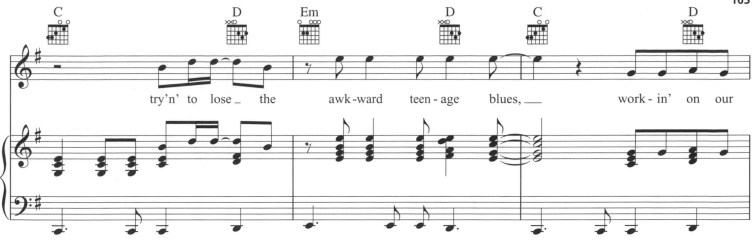

try'n' to lose _ the awk-ward teen-age blues, ___ work-in' on our

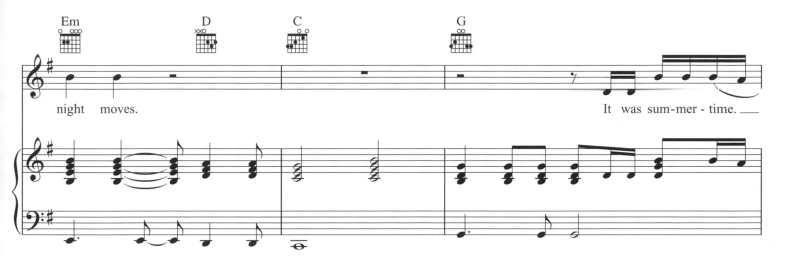

night moves. It was sum-mer - time. ___

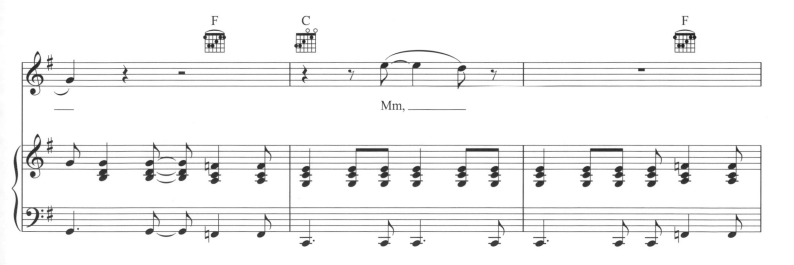

Mm, _____

sweet _ sum-mer - time, sum-mer - time.

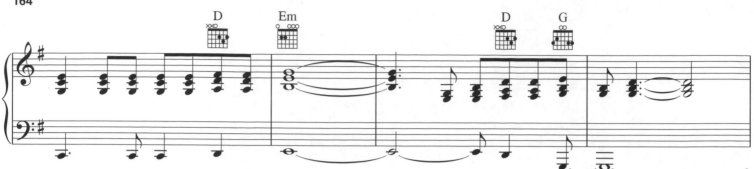

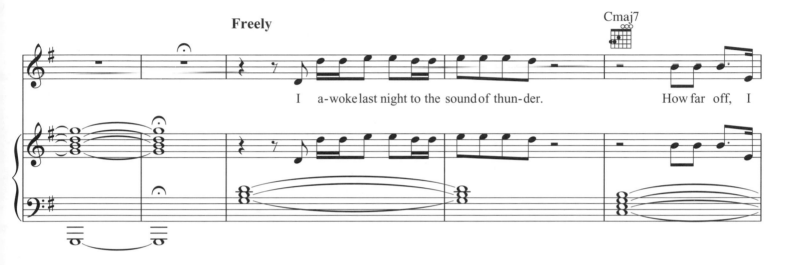

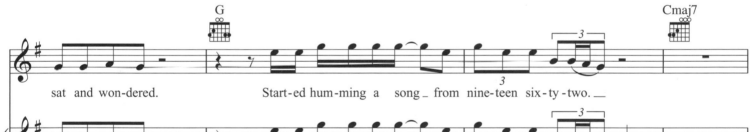

Tempo I

Strange how the night moves, ___ with au-tumn clos-ing in. ___

Night moves.

Lead vocal ad lib. to end

Night moves.

1–7

8

SOUTHERN CROSS

Words and Music by STEPHEN STILLS,
RICHARD CURTIS and MICHAEL CURTIS

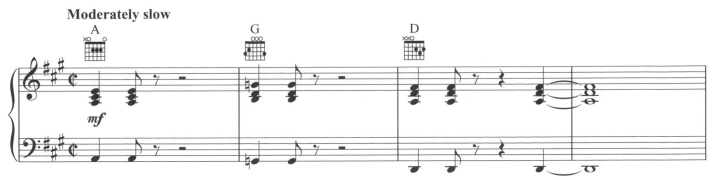

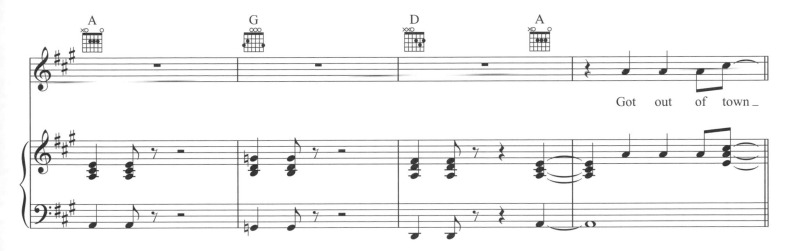

Got out of town

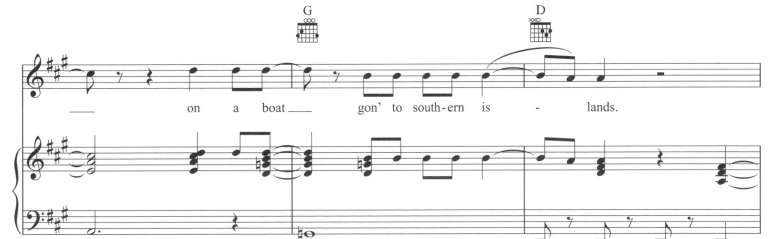

on a boat gon' to south-ern is - lands.

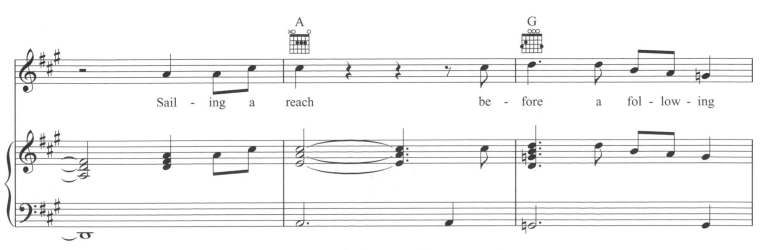

Sail - ing a reach before a fol - low - ing

sea.   She was mak - ing for the trades _

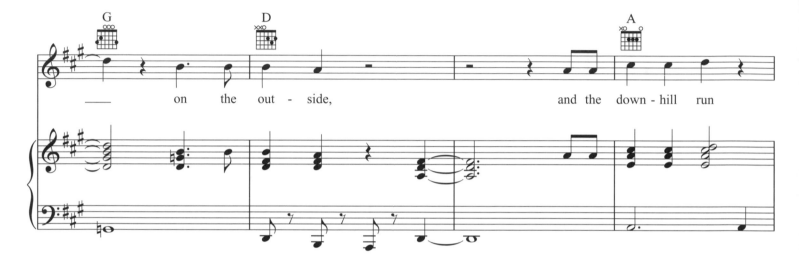

____ on the out - side,   and the down - hill run

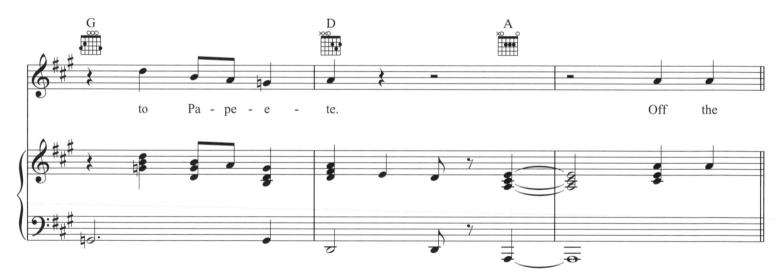

to Pa - pe - e - te.   Off the

wind   on   this   head - ing, lie ____ the Mar - que - sas.
sail - ing   for   to - mor - row. My dreams are a - dy - ing.

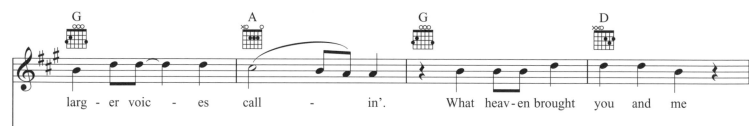

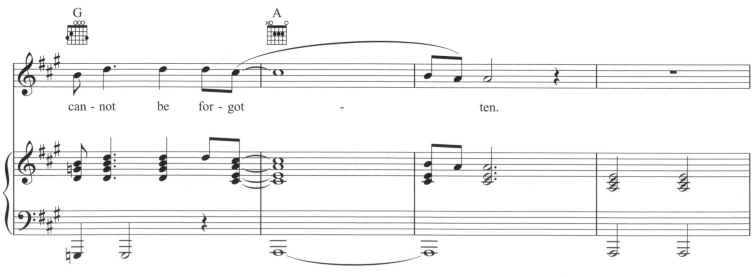

I have been a - round _____ the world,

look - in' for that wom - an - girl

who knows love can en - dure.

And you know it will. ____

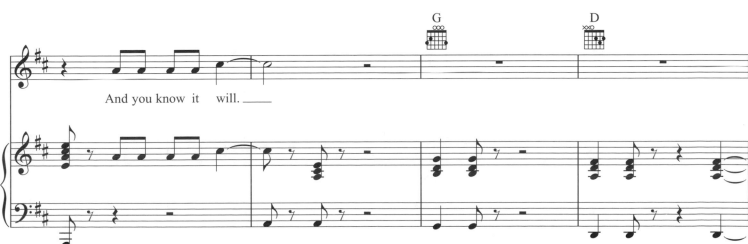

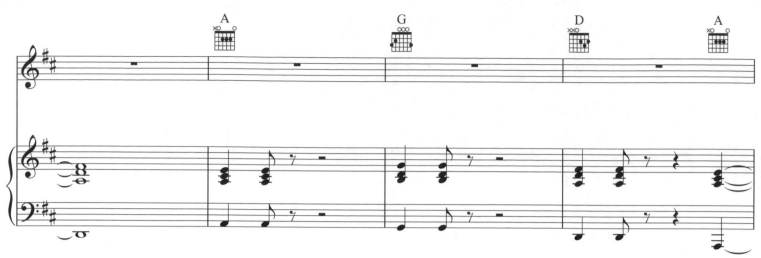

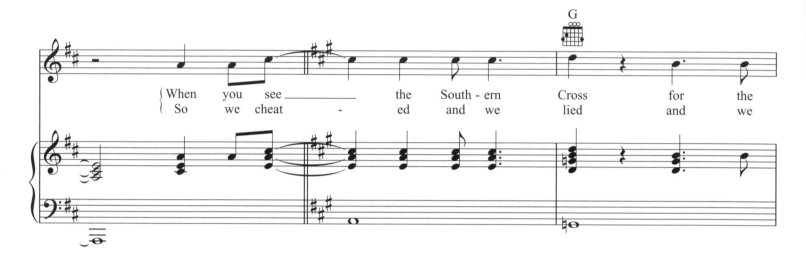

When you see _____ the South-ern Cross for the
So we cheat - ed and we lied for and we

first time,
test - ed.
you un-der-stand _ now why you came _ this
And we nev-er failed to fail; it was _ the

way.
eas - i - est thing to do.
'Cause the truth you might _ be run-nin' from is
You will _ sur - vive be - ing

so small, / best - ed.

but it's as big as the prom - ise, / Some - bod - y fine will come a - long, make me for-

prom - ise of a com - in' day. / get a - bout lov - ing you

So _____ I'm / in the South - ern

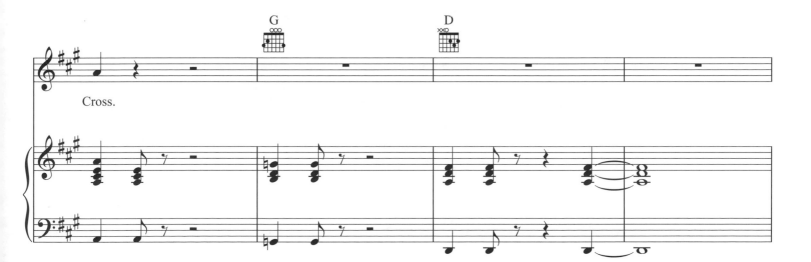

Cross.

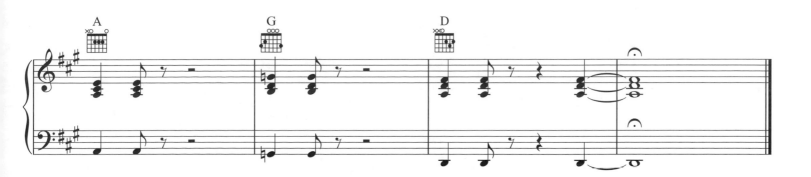

NORWEGIAN WOOD
(This Bird Has Flown)

Words and Music by JOHN LENNON
and PAUL McCARTNEY

Moderately

I once had a girl, or should I say she once had me.

Instrumental

She showed me her room, is-n't it good Nor-we-gian wood. She

End instrumental

She

asked me to stay and she told me to sit an-y-where. So

told me she worked in the morn-ing and start-ed to laugh. I

I looked a - round and I no - ticed there was - n't a chair.
told her I did - n't and crawled off to sleep in the bath.

I sat on a rug, bid - ing my time, drink - ing her wine.
And when I a - woke I was a - lone; this bird had flown.

We talked un - til two and then she said, "It's time for bed."
So I lit a fire, is - n't it good Nor - we - gian wood.

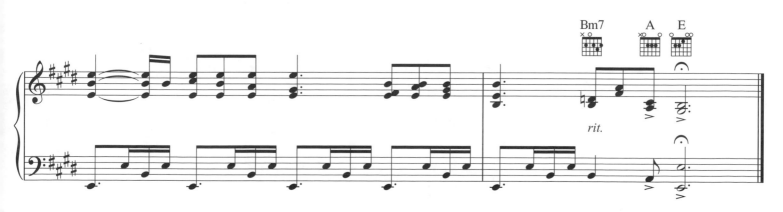

rit.

PLEASE COME TO BOSTON

Words and Music by
DAVE LOGGINS

Moderately fast

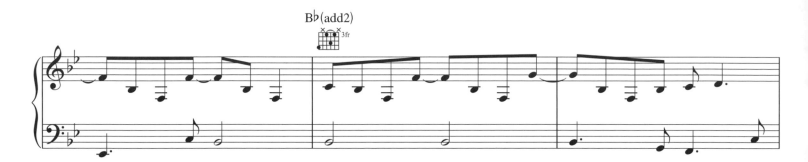

He said please come to Bos - ton for __ the spring -
please come to Den - ver with __ the snow -
please come to L. A. __ to live __ for - ev - er

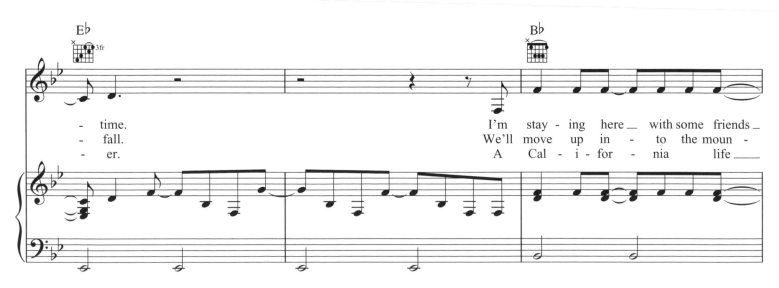

- time.
- fall.
- er.

I'm stay - ing here __ with some friends __
We'll move up in - to the moun -
A Cal - i - for - nia life

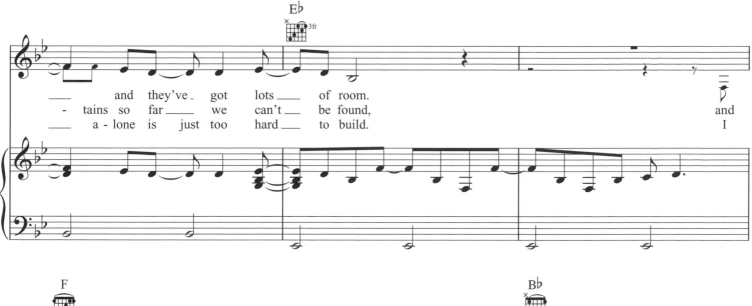

and they've got lots ___ of room.
- tains so far ___ we can't ___ be found,
___ a - lone is just too hard ___ to build.

and
I

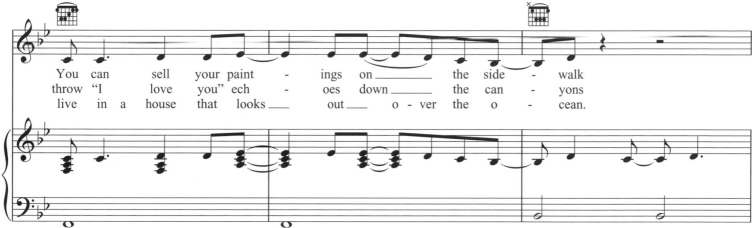

You can sell your paint - ings on ___ the side - walk
throw "I love you" ech - oes down ___ the can - yons
live in a house that looks ___ out ___ o - ver the o - cean.

by a ca - fé where I hope ___ to be work - in' soon. ___
and then lie a - wake at night ___ un - til they come back a - round.
And there's some stars that fell from the sky liv - in' up on the hill. ___

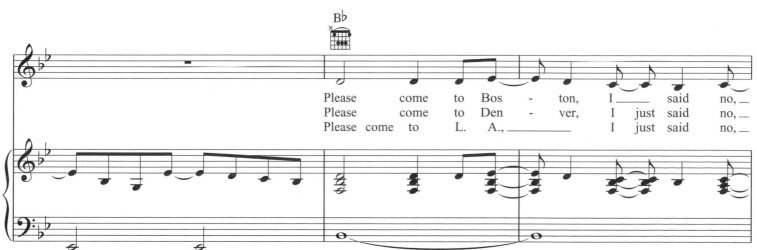

Please come to Bos - ton, I ___ said no, ___
Please come to Den - ver, I just said no, ___
Please come to L. A., ___ I just said no, ___

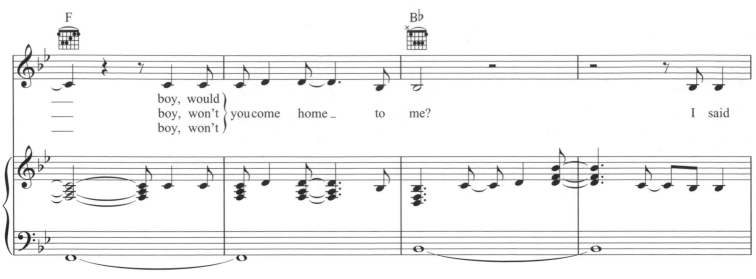

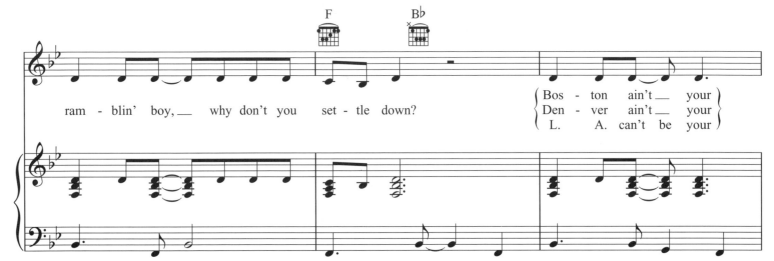

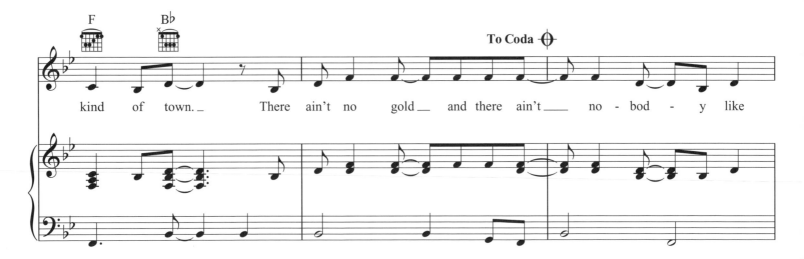

He said

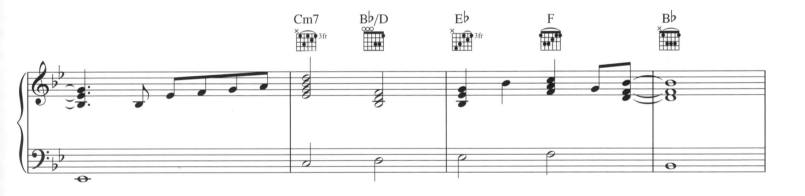

Now that drift-er's world goes 'round and 'round and I doubt

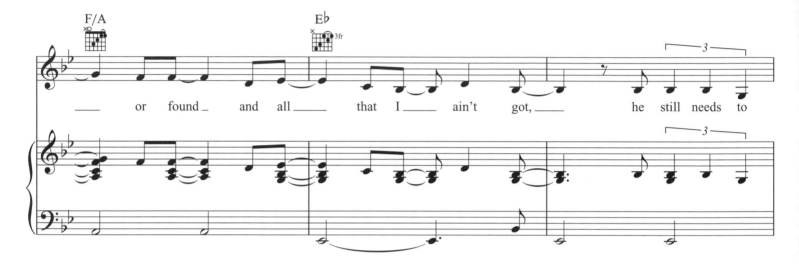

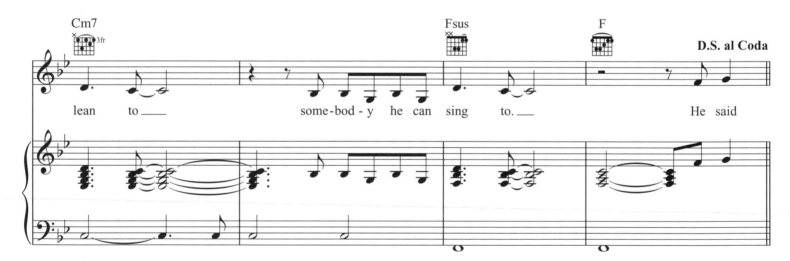

from Ten-nes-see.

I'm the num-ber one fan of the man

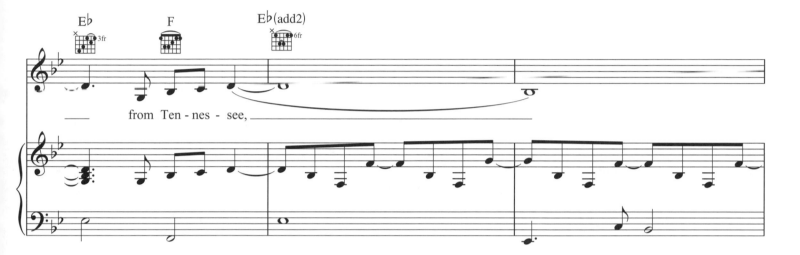

from Ten-nes-see,

Ten-nes-see.

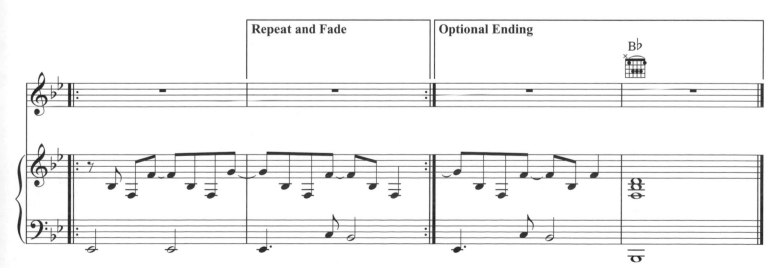

Repeat and Fade

Optional Ending

SUMMER BREEZE

Words and Music by JAMES SEALS
and DASH CROFTS

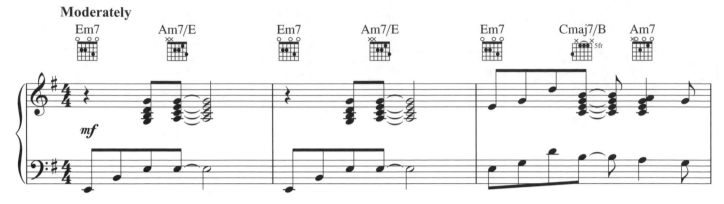

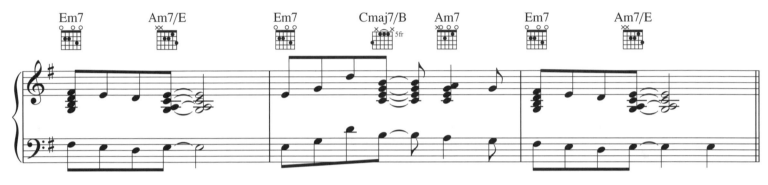

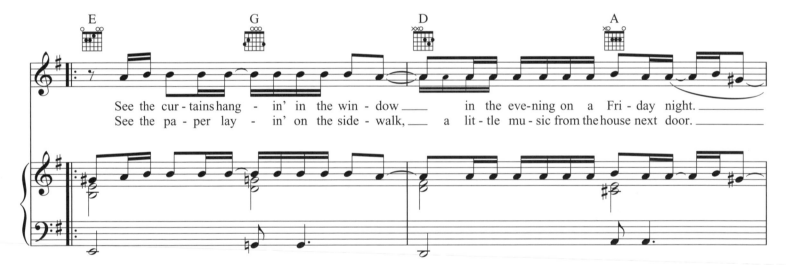

See the cur - tains hang - in' in the win - dow ___ in the eve - ning on a Fri - day night. ___
See the pa - per lay - in' on the side - walk, ___ a lit - tle mu - sic from the house next door. ___

A lit - tle light a - shin - in' through the win - dow
So I walk on up to the door - step, ___

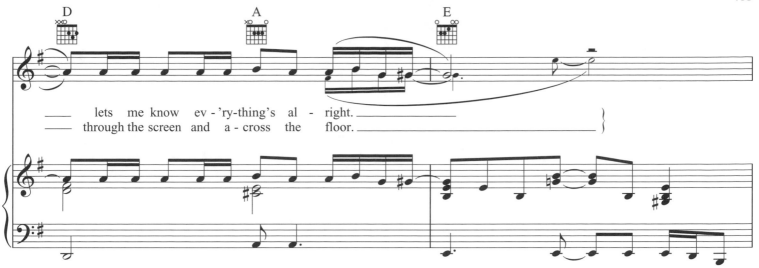

lets me know ev-'ry-thing's al - right. _____
through the screen and a-cross the floor. _____

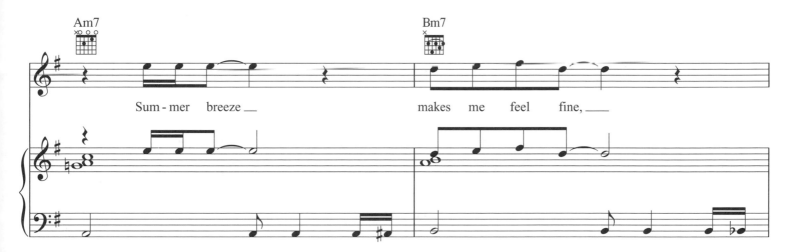

Sum - mer breeze ___ makes me feel fine, ___

blow - in' through the jas - mine in my mind. _____

Sum - mer breeze ___

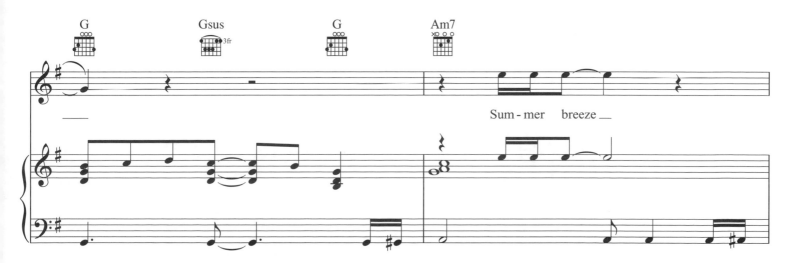

makes me feel fine, ___ blow - in' through the jas - mine in my

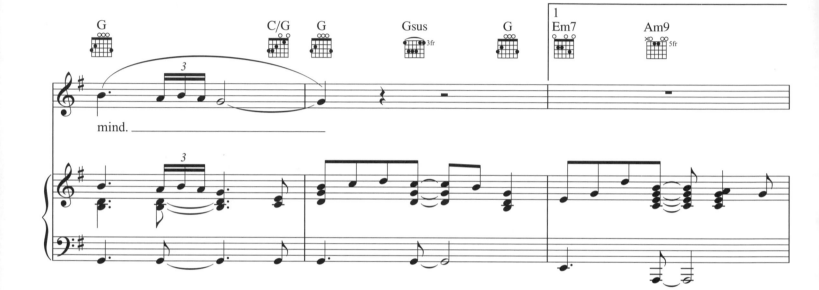

mind. _____

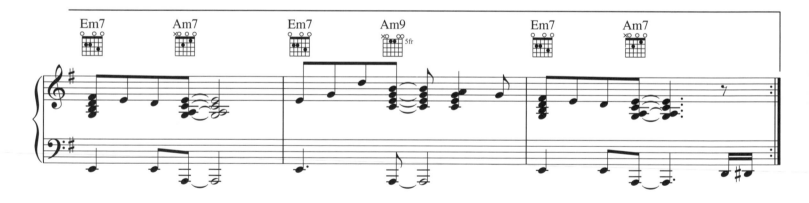

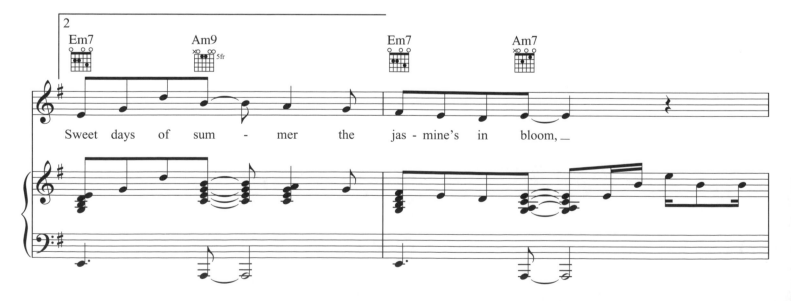

Sweet days of sum - mer the jas - mine's in bloom, _

Ju - ly is dressed __ up and play - ing her tune. __ When I come

home __ from a hard _____ day's work __ and you're

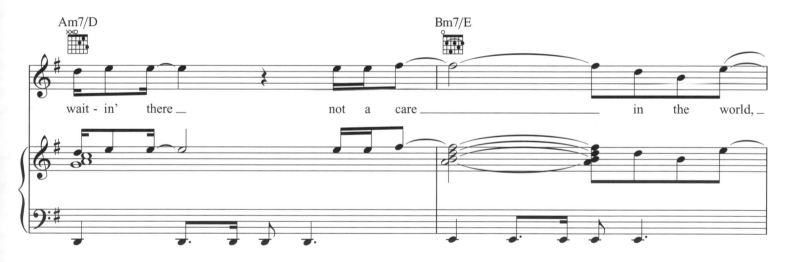

wait - in' there __ not a care _____ in the world, __

see the smile a - wait - in' in the kitch - en,

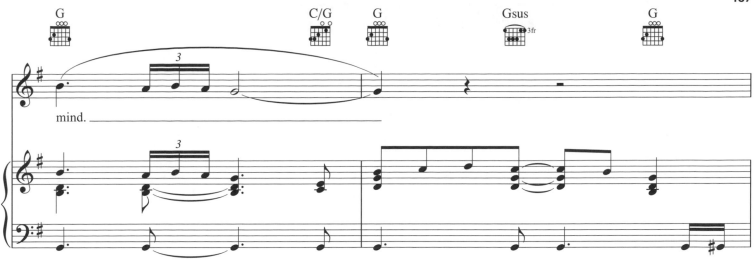

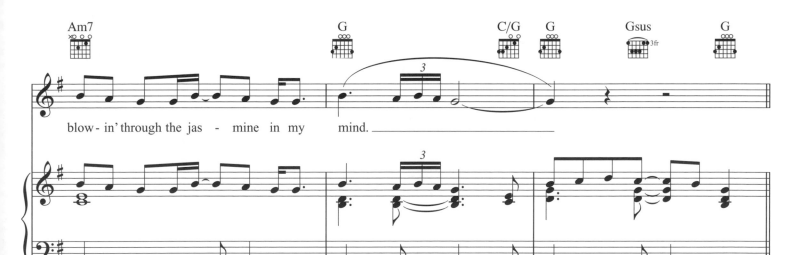

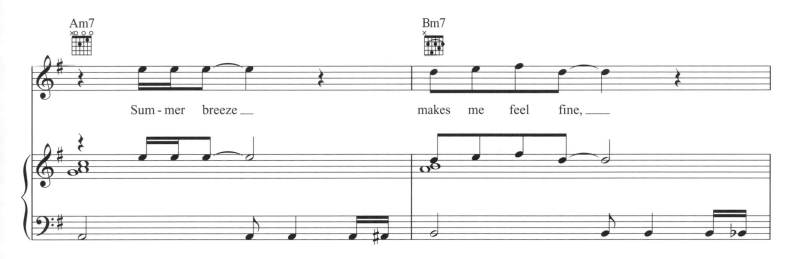

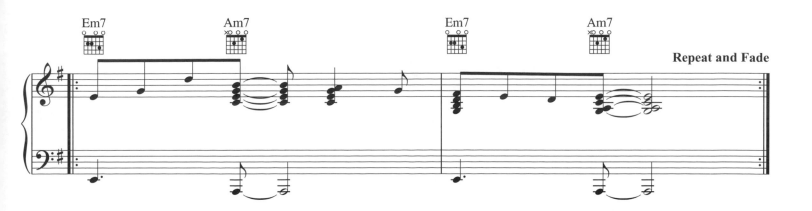

TEARS IN HEAVEN

Words and Music by ERIC CLAPTON
and WILL JENNINGS

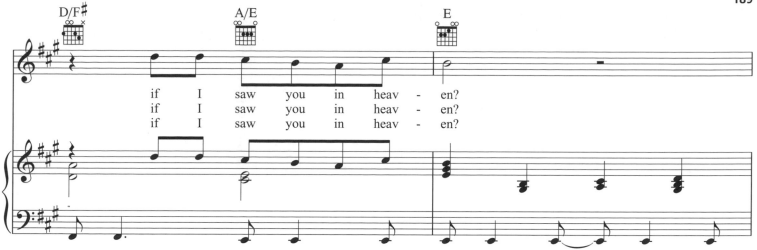

if I saw you in heav - en?
if I saw you in heav - en?
if I saw you in heav - en?

(1., 3.) I must be strong ___ and car - ry on ___
(2.) I'll find my way ___ through night and day ___

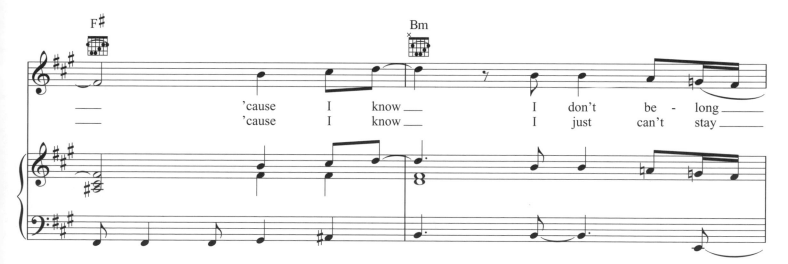

___ 'cause I know ___ I don't be - long ___
___ 'cause I know ___ I just can't stay ___

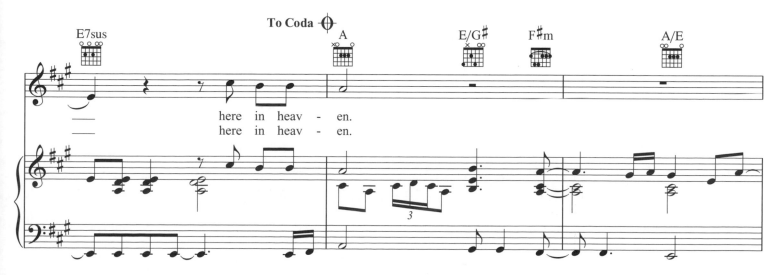

___ here in heav - en.
___ here in heav - en.

Time can bring you down, _____

_____ time can bend your knees. _____

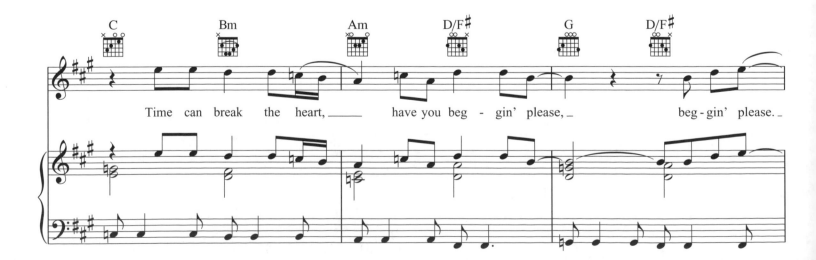

Time can break the heart, _____ have you beg - gin' please, _ beg - gin' please. _

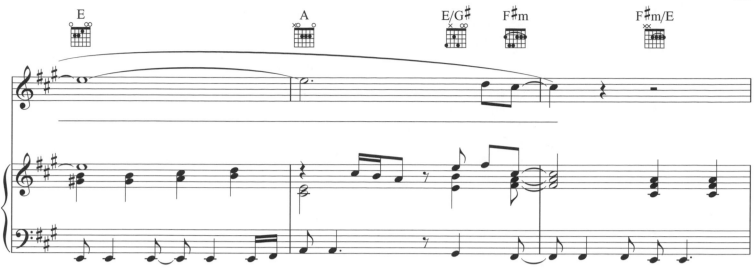

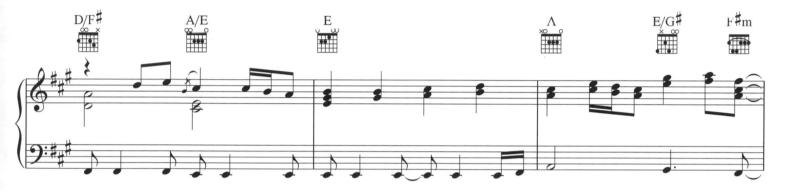

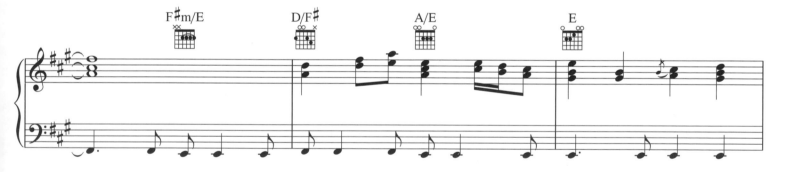

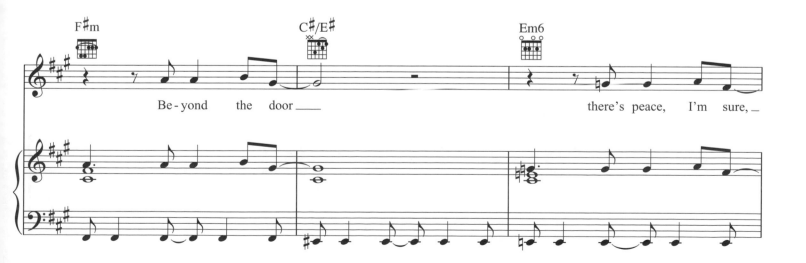

Be-yond the door ____ there's peace, I'm sure, __

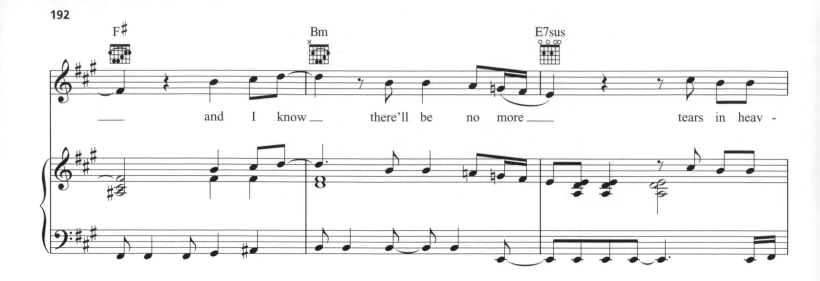

and I know ___ there'll be no more ___ tears in heav-

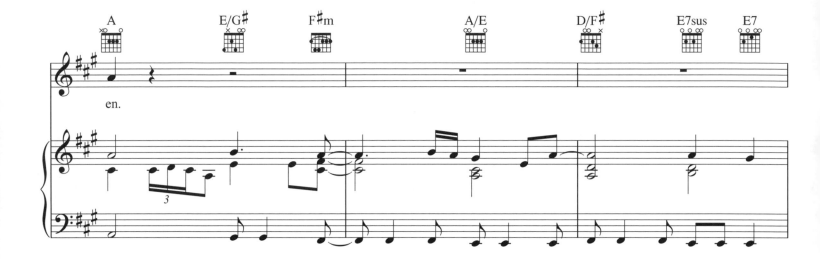

en.

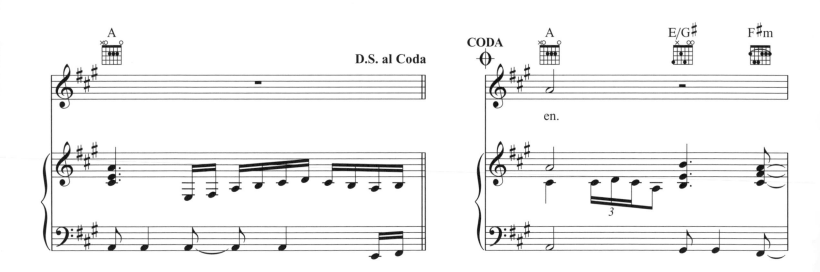

D.S. al Coda

CODA

en.

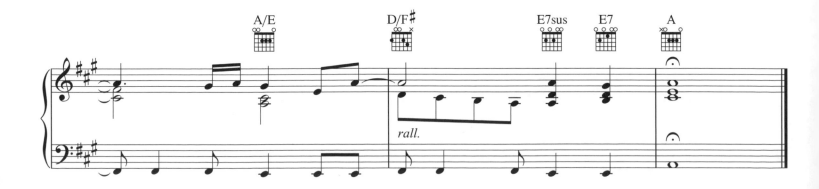

rall.

WISH YOU WERE HERE

Words and Music by ROGER WATERS
and DAVID GILMOUR

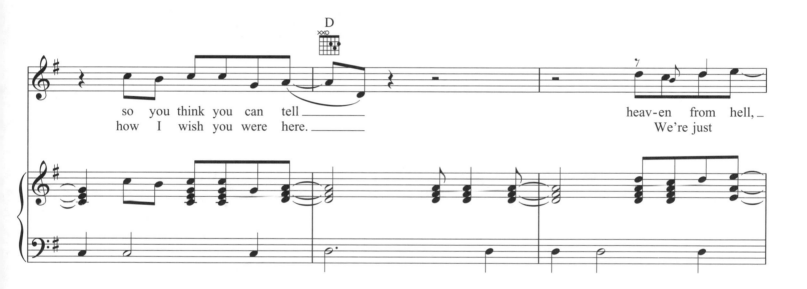

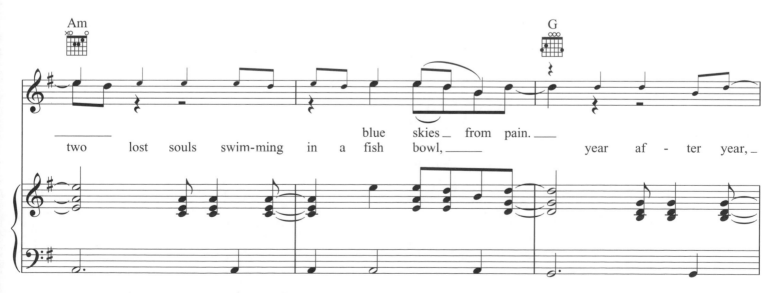

Can you tell a green field _____ run-ning o - ver the same ___ old ground. from a cold, steel

rail, _____ What have we found? _____ a smile ___ from a veil, The same old ___ fears. _____

To Coda ⊕

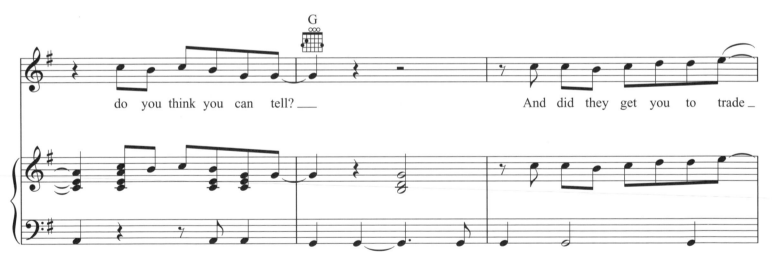

do you think you can tell? ___ And did they get you to trade ___

_____ your he - roes for ghosts, ___

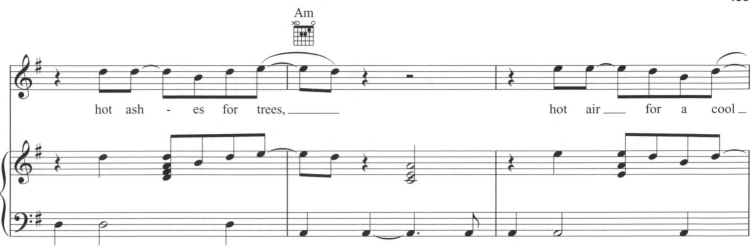

hot ash-es for trees, _____ hot air ___ for a cool ___

_____ breeze, _ cold ___ com-fort for change? _____

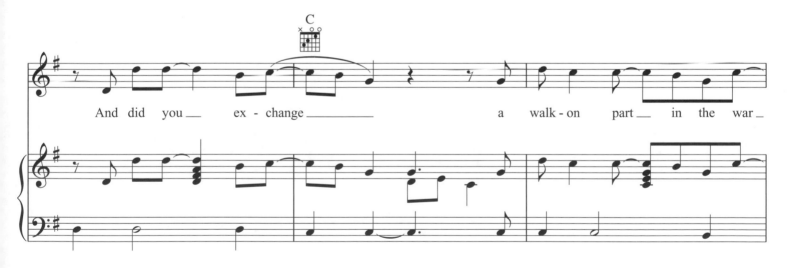

And did you ___ ex-change _____ a walk-on part ___ in the war _

___ for a lead ____ role in a cage? _____

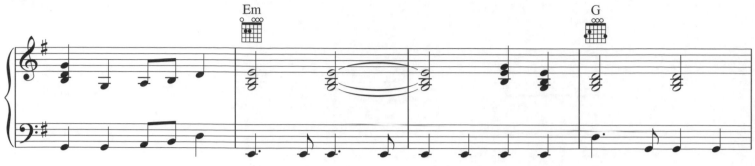

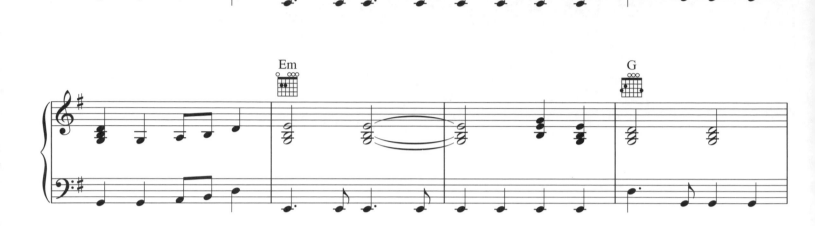

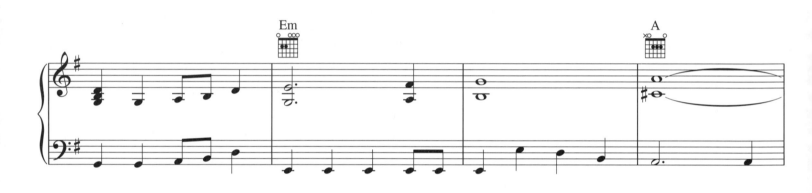

Wish you __ were __ here. _____

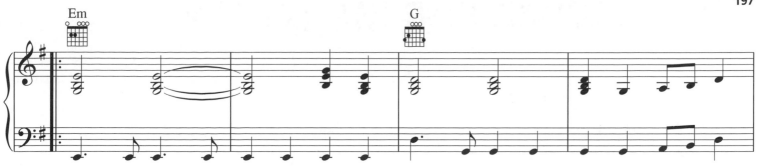

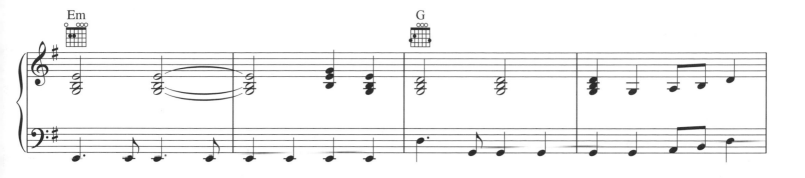

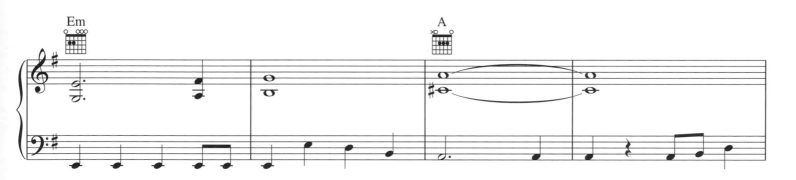

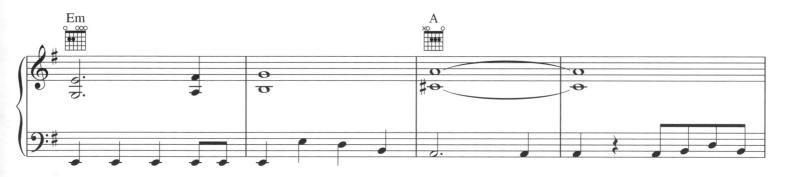

Da da da da   da da da da da.

TIME FOR ME TO FLY

Words and Music by
KEVIN CRONIN

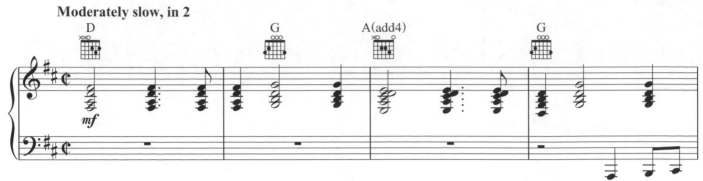

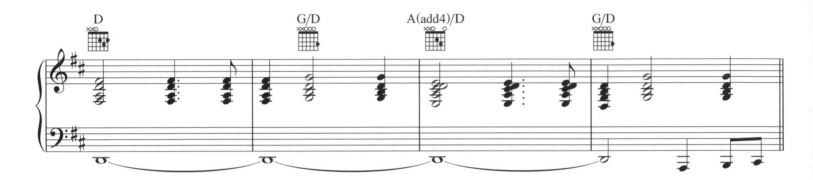

I've been a-round ___ for you, been up and down ___ for ___ you; but
You said we'd work ___ it out. You said that you had ___ no ___ doubt that

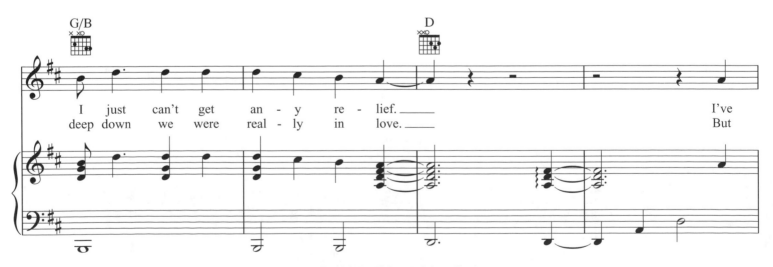

I just can't get an-y re-lief. ___ I've
deep down we were real-ly in love. ___ But

swal - lowed my pride ____ for you, lived and lied ____ for __ you; but
I'm tired of hold - ing on to a feel - ing I know ____ is __ gone. I

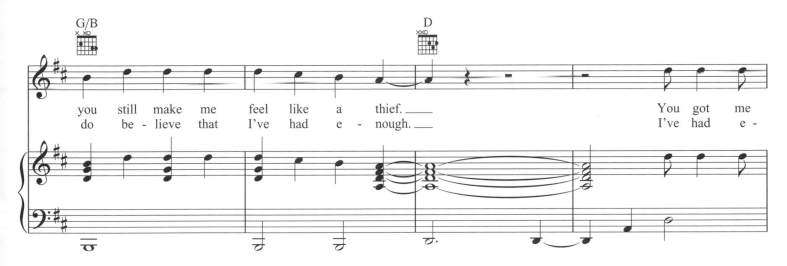

you still make me feel like a thief. ____ You got me
do be - lieve that I've had e - nough. ____ I've had e -

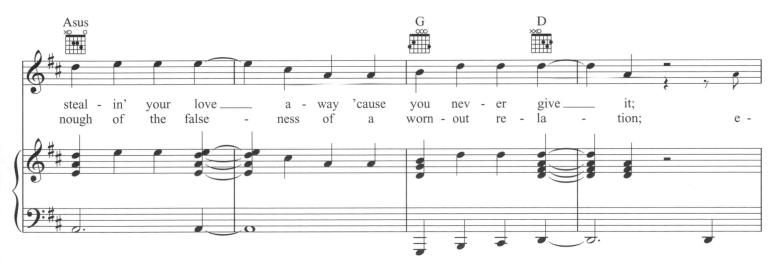

steal - in' your love ____ a - way 'cause you nev - er give ____ it;
nough of the false - ness of a worn - out re - la - tion;

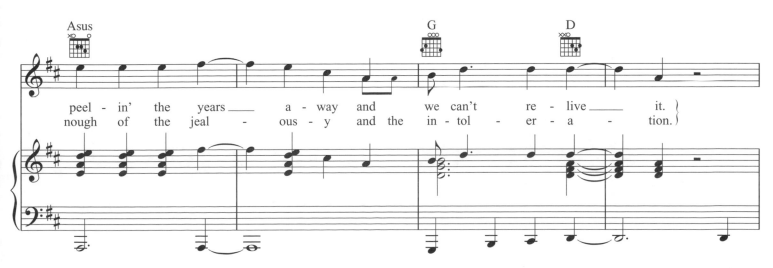

peel - in' the years ____ a - way and we can't re - live ____ it.
nough of the jeal - ous - y and the in - tol - er - a - tion.

I make you laugh, _____ and you make me cry. _____

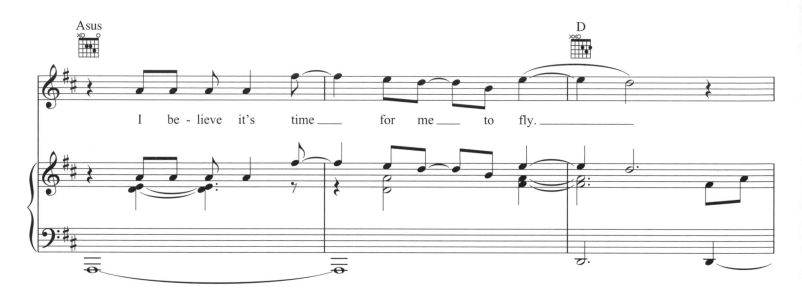

I be-lieve it's time ___ for me ___ to fly. _____

Time for me ___ to fly. _____ I've got to set ___ my-self free.

Time for me___ to fly._____ That's just how it's___ got to___ be.___

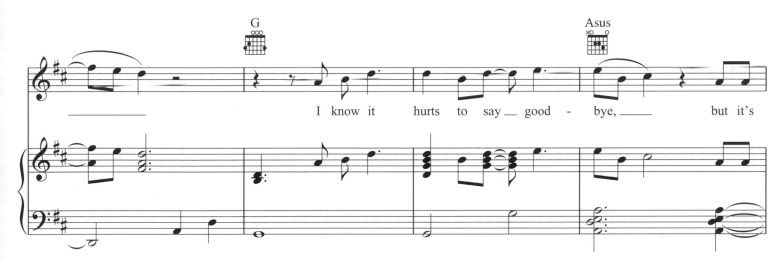

_____ I know it hurts to say___ good - bye,_____ but it's

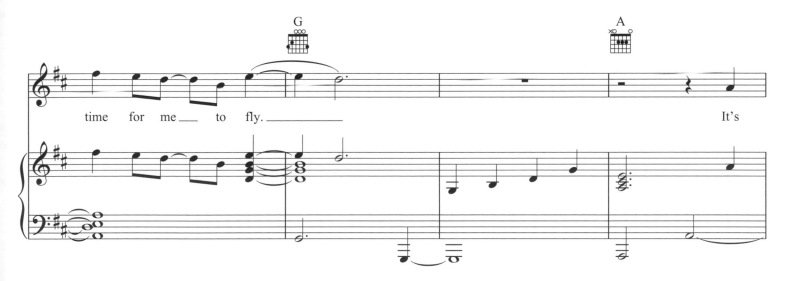

time for me___ to fly._____ It's

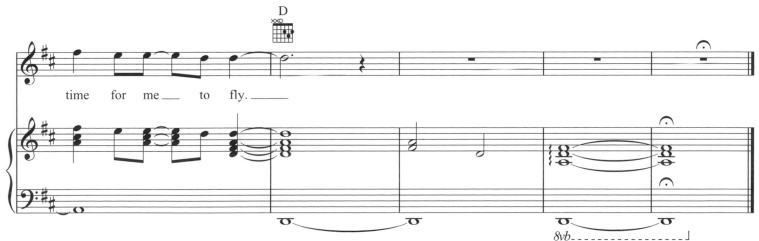

time for me___ to fly._____

TIME IN A BOTTLE

Words and Music by
JIM CROCE

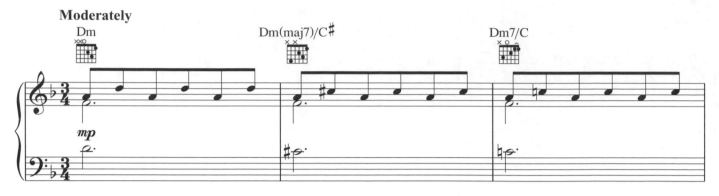

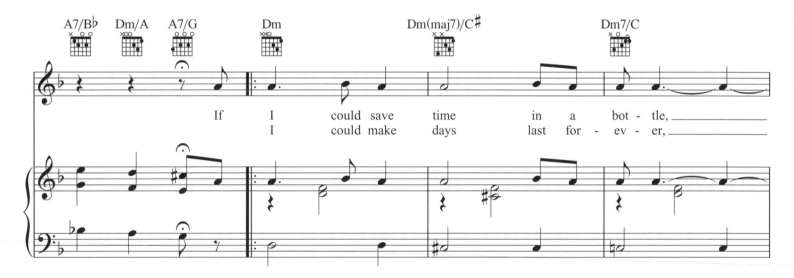

If I could save time in a bot - tle, ____
I could make days last for - ev - er, ____

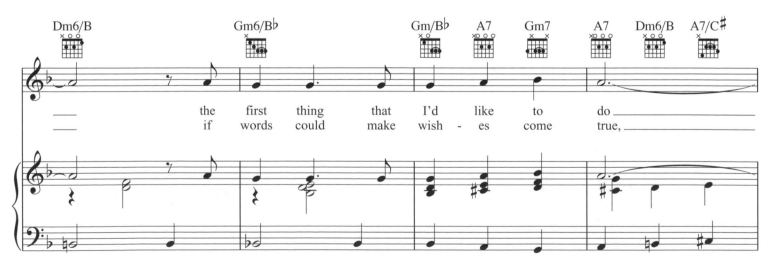

____ the first thing that I'd like to do ____
____ if words could make wish - es come true, ____

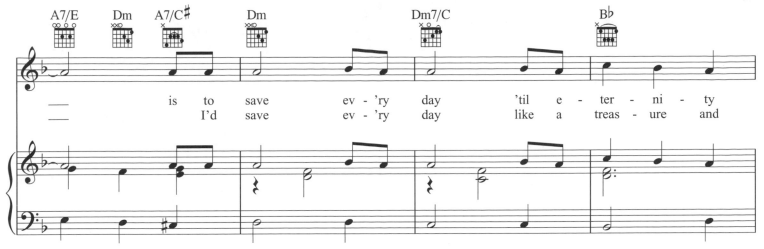

is to save ev-'ry day 'til e - ter - ni - ty
I'd save ev-'ry day like a treas - ure and

pass - es a - way just to spend them with you.
then a - gain I would spend them with you.

If ___ But there nev - er seems to

be e - nough time to do the things you want to do once you

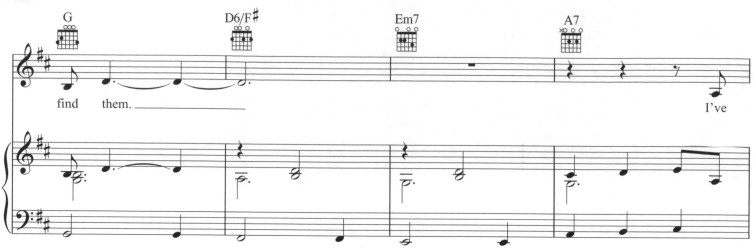

find them. _____ I've

looked a-round e-nough to know that you're the one I want to go through

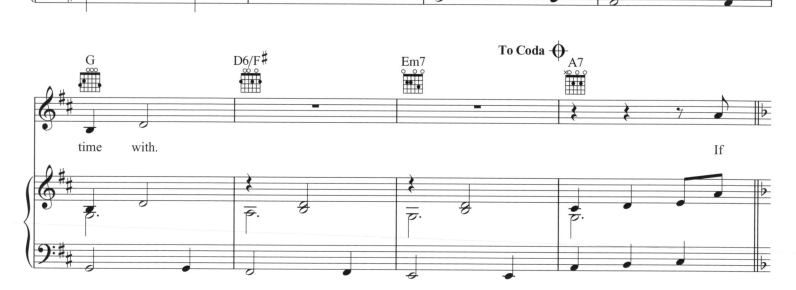

time with. If

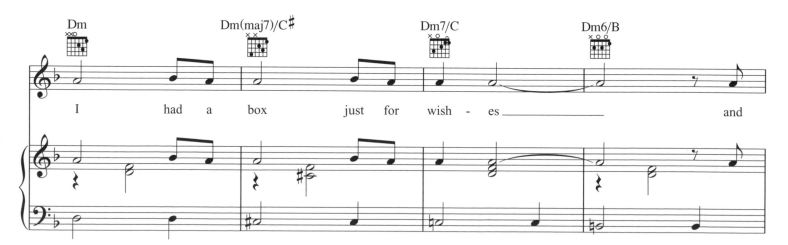

I had a box just for wish-es _____ and

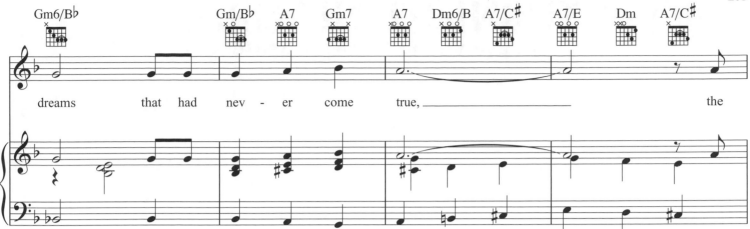

dreams that had nev - er come true, _____ the

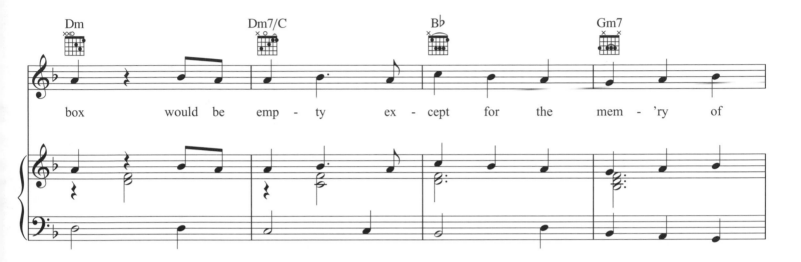

box would be emp - ty ex - cept for the mem - 'ry of

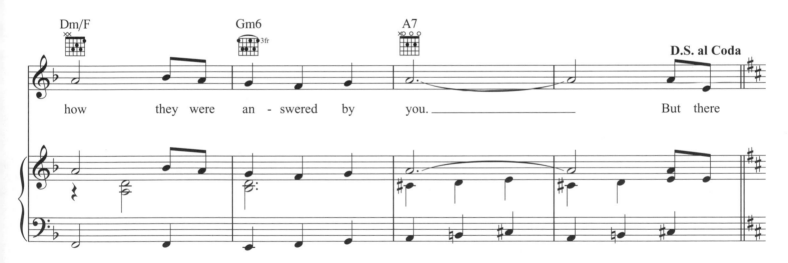

how they were an - swered by you. _____ But there

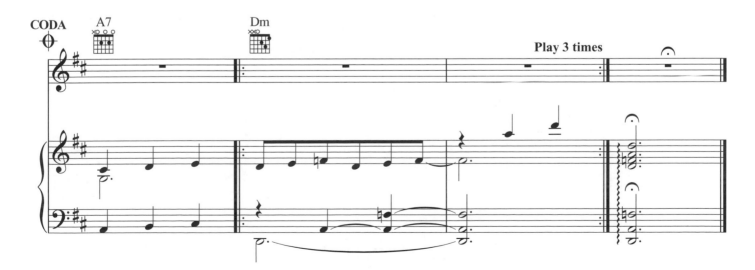

TURN! TURN! TURN!
(To Everything There Is a Season)

Words from the Book of Ecclesiastes
Adaptation and Music by PETE SEEGER

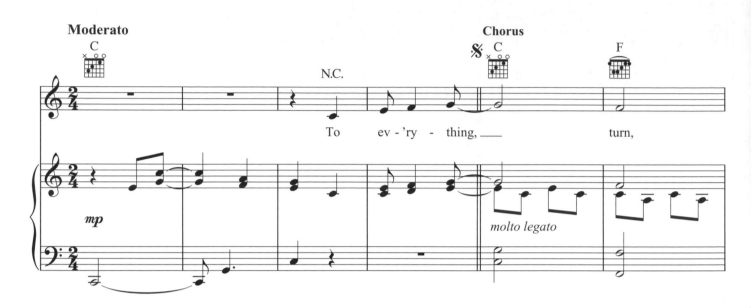

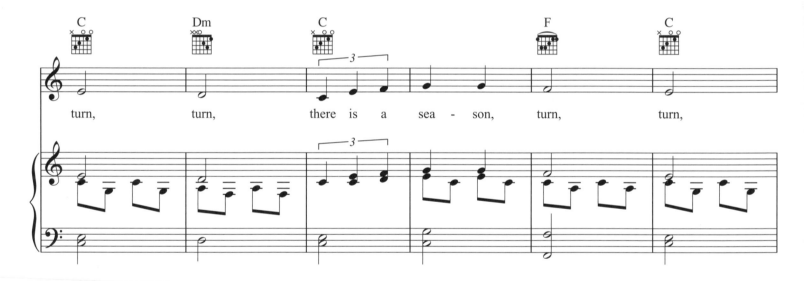

Verse 1

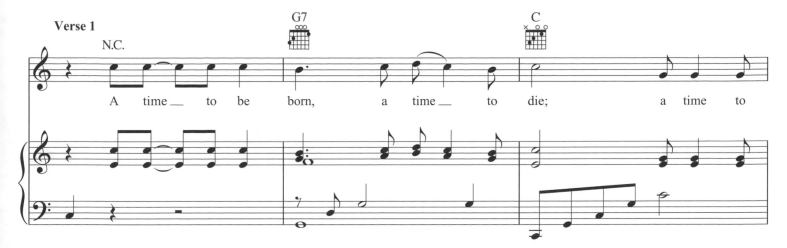

A time _ to be born, a time _ to die; a time to

plant, a time _ to reap; a time to kill, a time _ to heal; a time to

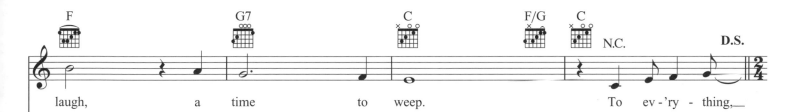

laugh, a time to weep. To ev-'ry-thing,_

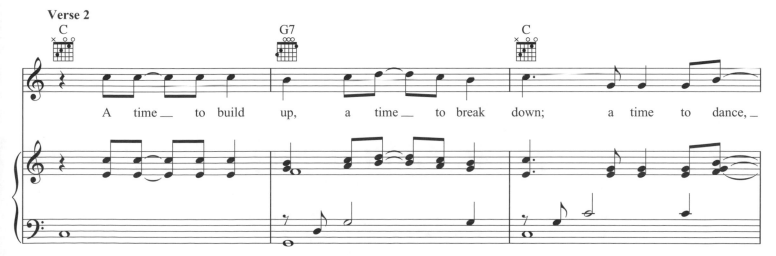

Verse 2

A time _ to build up, a time _ to break down; a time to dance, _

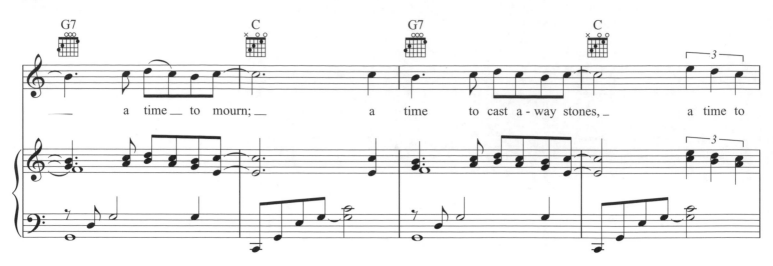

a time __ to mourn; __ a time to cast a-way stones, __ a time to

gath-er __ stones __ to-geth-er. __ To ev-'ry-thing, __

Verse 3

A time __ of love, __ a time __ of hate; a time of war, __ a time __ of

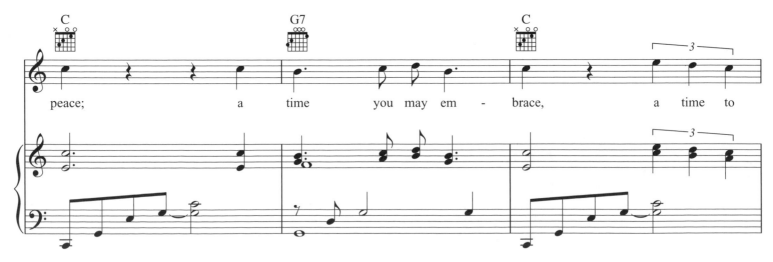

peace; a time you may em-brace, a time to

re-frain _____ from em-brac-ing. _____ To ev-'ry-thing, ___

Verse 4

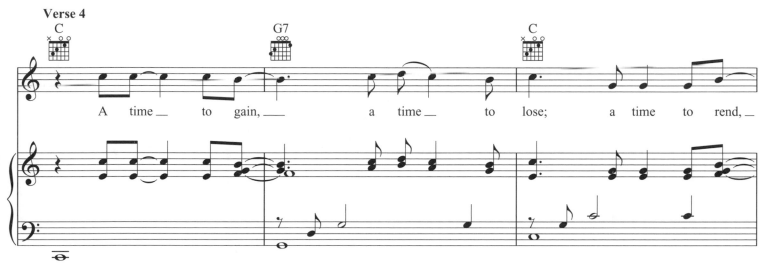

A time ___ to gain, ___ a time ___ to lose; a time to rend, ___

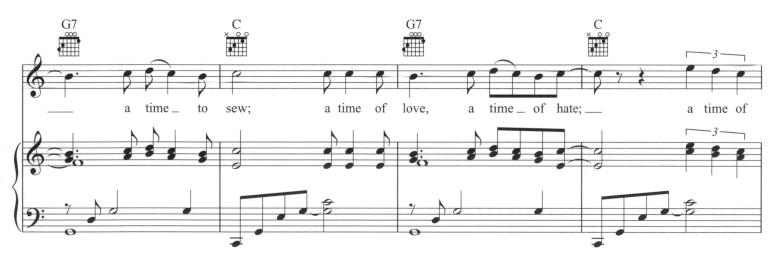

___ a time ___ to sew; a time of love, a time ___ of hate; ___ a time of

peace, I swear it's not too late. ___ To ev-'ry-thing, ___

TWO OUT OF THREE AIN'T BAD

Words and Music by
JIM STEINMAN

Moderately slow, with a beat

Ba - by, we can talk all ___ night, ___

but that ain't get-ting us no - where.   I've told you ev - 'ry-thing I

pos - si - bly can; ___ there's noth-ing left in - side ___ of here.   And

may-be you can cry all __ night, __ but that-'ll nev-er change __ the way __

__ that I feel. __ The snow is real-ly pil-ing up out - side; __ I

wish you would-n't make __ me leave __ here. I poured it on and I poured __

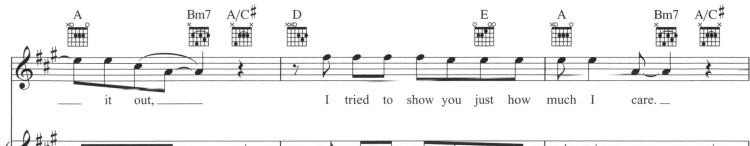

__ it out, __ I tried to show you just how much I care. __

I'm tired of words and I'm too hoarse to shout, ___ but you've been cold to

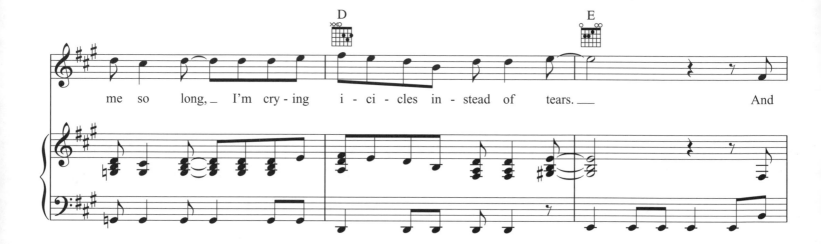

me so long, ___ I'm cry-ing i-ci-cles in-stead of tears. ___ And

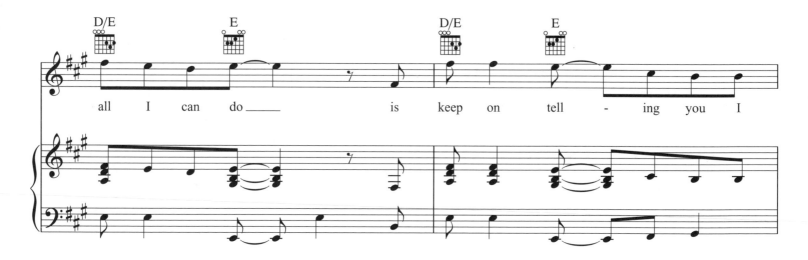

all I can do ___ is keep on tell-ing you I

want you, ___ I need you, ___ but there ain't no way ___ I'm ev-

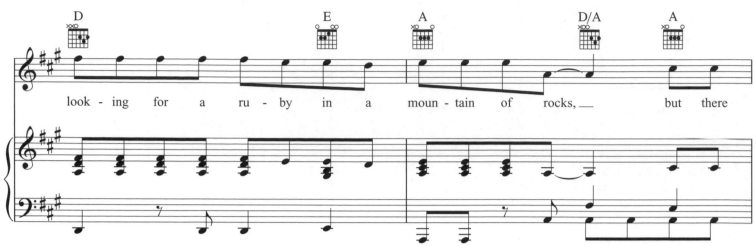

look - ing for a ru - by in a moun - tain of rocks, ___ but there

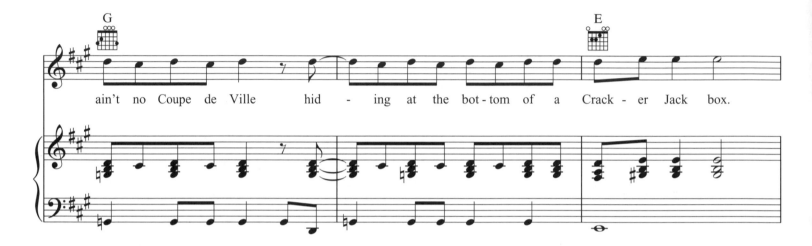

ain't no Coupe de Ville hid - ing at the bot - tom of a Crack - er Jack box.

I can't lie. I can't tell you that I'm

some - thing I'm not, ___ no mat - ter how I try. I'll nev - er be a - ble

to give you some-thing, some-thing that I just have-n't got. ___ There's

on - ly one girl __ that I will ev - er love, and that was so man - y years _ a - go. ___

___ And though I know I'll nev - er get her out of my heart, _ she nev - er

loved me back, _ ooh, _____ I know. _ Well, I re - mem - ber how she left me on a

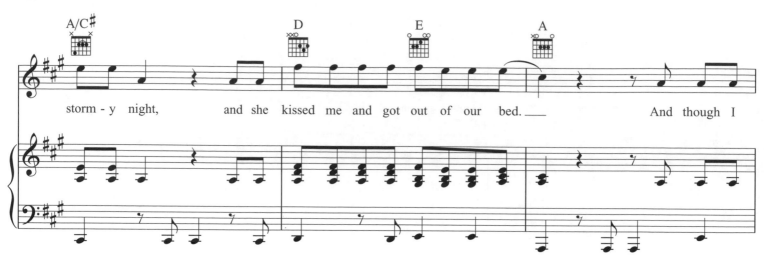

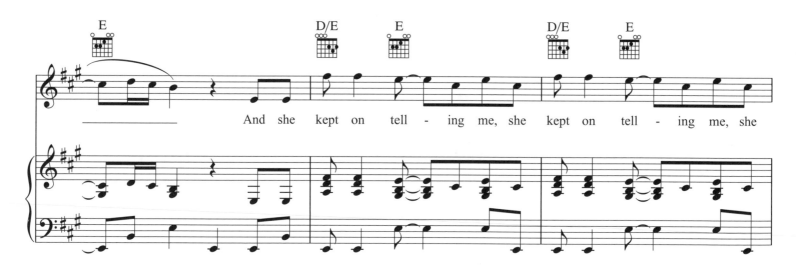

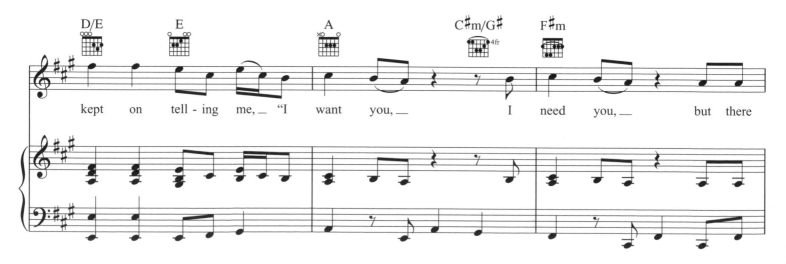

WORKING CLASS HERO

Words and Music by
JOHN LENNON

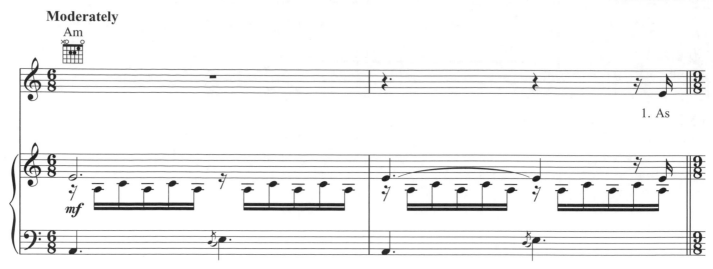

soon as you're born, ___ they make you feel small ___
2. hurt you at home and they hit you at school. ___
3. tor-tured and scared you for twen-ty odd years, ___
4., 5. *(See additional lyrics)*

by giv-ing you no time in-stead of it all, ___
They hate you if you're clev-er and they de-spise a fool, ___
then they ex-pect you to pick a ca-reer. ___

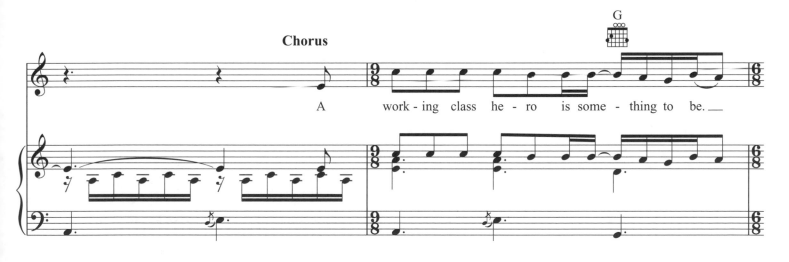

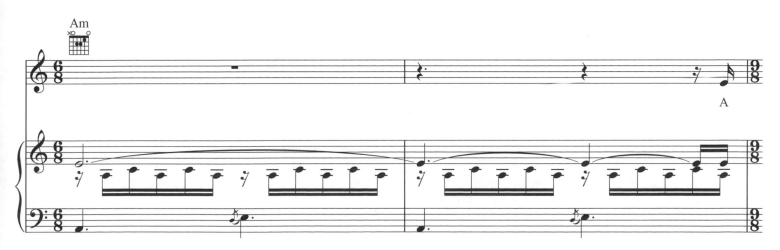

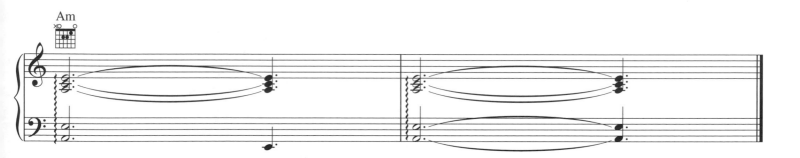

Additional Lyrics

4. Keep you doped with religion and sex and TV.
   And you think you're so clever and classless and free.
   But you're still fucking peasants as far as I can see.
   Chorus

5. There's room at the top they are telling you still.
   But first you must learn how to smile as you kill
   If you want to be like the folks on the hill.
   Chorus

YESTERDAY

Words and Music by JOHN LENNON
and PAUL McCARTNEY

Moderately, with expression

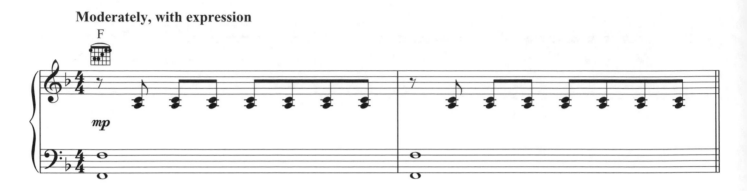

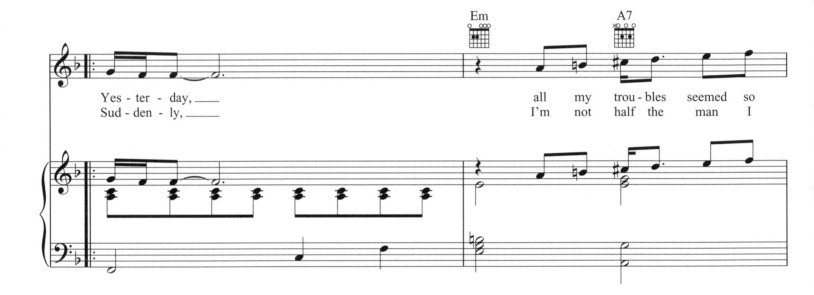

Yes - ter - day, _____ all my trou - bles seemed so
Sud - den - ly, _____ I'm not half the man I

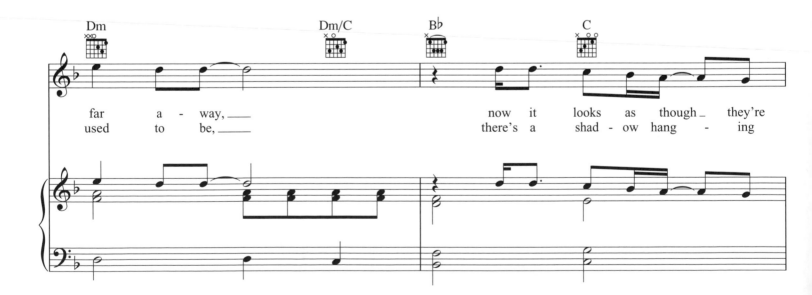

far a - way, _____ now it looks as though _ they're
used to be, _____ there's a shad - ow hang - ing

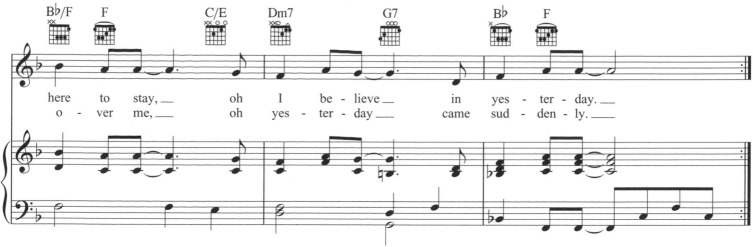

here to stay, __ oh I be - lieve __ in yes - ter - day. __
o - ver me, __ oh yes - ter - day __ came sud - den - ly. __

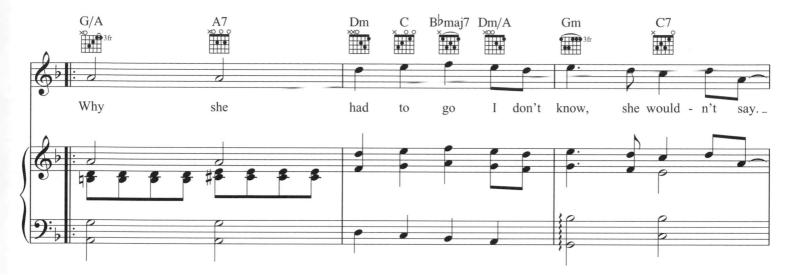

Why she had to go I don't know, she would - n't say. __

I said

some - thing wrong, now I long for yes - ter - day.

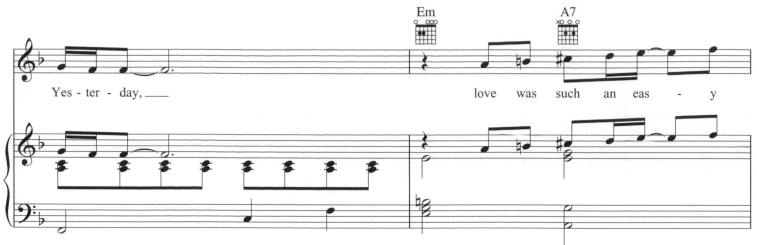

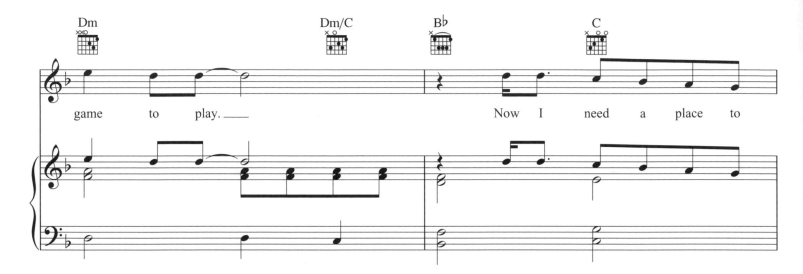

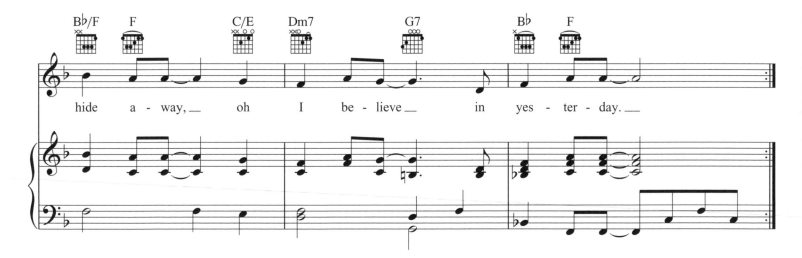

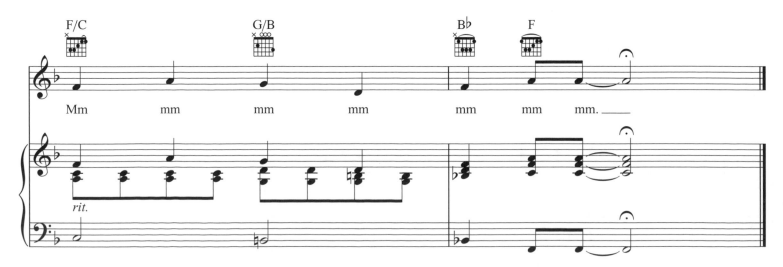